For Yvonne

THE GREAT LEGAL REFORMATION

NOTES FROM THE FIELD

Also by Mitchell Kowalski

*Avoiding Extinction: Reimagining Legal
Services for the 21st Century*

THE GREAT LEGAL REFORMATION

NOTES FROM THE FIELD

MITCHELL KOWALSKI

THE GREAT LEGAL REFORMATION
NOTES FROM THE FIELD

iUniverse books may be ordered through booksellers or by contacting:

iUniverse
1663 Liberty Drive
Bloomington, IN 47403
www.iuniverse.com
1-800-Authors (1-800-288-4677)

ISBN: 978-1-5320-3216-5 (sc)
ISBN: 978-1-5320-3218-9 (hc)
ISBN: 978-1-5320-3217-2 (e)

Library of Congress Control Number: 2017913330

Print information available on the last page.

iUniverse rev. date: 09/15/2017

People who say it cannot be done should not interrupt those who are doing it.

- George Bernard Shaw

CONTENTS

PREFACE

There are a growing number of commentators who suggest that we are now at the tipping point of change in legal services; the beginning of what I call the Great Legal Reformation. In blogs, Twitter, and other digital modes, they speak of OldLaw, EngagedLaw, NextLaw, NewLaw, Smarter Law, Legal by Design, T-shaped lawyers, and the Golden Age of Legal Entrepreneurs. They say that without significant reform, the legal profession will be unable to cope with an onslaught of new competitors, many of whom are not lawyers; that the profession's love affair with precedent, combined with risk aversion and an unwillingness to be a first mover, will form a deadly cocktail for many. And if that is so, perhaps the antidote is to shine a light on those who are best adjusting to the Great Legal Reformation.

This book shares the stories of interesting and instructive adaptations to the Great Legal Reformation, so as to provide guidance and inspiration to those coming next. The subtitle, *Notes from the Field*, should alert readers that this is not an attempt to put together a comprehensive catalogue of every innovative legal services provider on the planet. There will be those whose stories are not shared in this book: ones that some will suggest should have been included. However, keeping up with the global legal marketplace is like drinking from a fire hose. At some point I had to stop gathering information, stop separating real innovation from hype, and focus on getting the book completed. Besides, there will undoubtedly be more books written about the Great Legal Reformation where those stories may appear.

Finally, much to the dismay of my accountant, none of the entities discussed in this book paid for "placement," nor did they pay any of the costs involved in this project. And while they were given an opportunity to comment on early drafts to ensure accuracy, all commentary and opinions are mine alone—as are any errors.

August 1, 2017
Toronto, Canada
Mitchell Kowalski

INTRODUCTION

"…a dangerous place from which to watch the world."

For many travelers, Wittenberg, Germany is just another quaint medieval town nestled along the Elbe River. It has the requisite colourful storefronts, cobblestoned streets, and impressive churches, as well as a town square that each December hosts a *Christkindlmarkt* overflowing with *gluhwein, marktchampignons,* and friendly locals. And like many small towns around the world, Wittenberg's population has been in steady decline. So much so that it's hard to imagine that at one time, this quiet town was once a bustling trade centre and seat of government, housing an important university and a monastery. It's harder still to imagine Wittenberg as the birthplace of one of Western civilization's greatest social, political, and religious upheavals: The Reformation.

Yet (according to legend) it was on October 31, 1517, that a former law-student-turned-obscure-monk named Martin Luther strode confidently up *Schlossstrasse* and nailed his famous 95 Theses to the door of the Castle Church; 95 "breathless bullet points, which ebb and flow between different aspects … [of selling salvation for past and future sins, called indulgences. Points which vacillate] … between outright condemnation and efforts at mitigation ..."[1] His timing could not have been better. Mechanical movable type printing was well established by 1517 and, with active printers in hundreds of towns across Central, Western, and Eastern Europe, copies of the 95 Theses (translated from Latin into German and then shortened to small pamphlets and even broadsheets) quickly spread across Europe. Friedrich Myconius, a friend of Luther, later wrote, "hardly 14 days had passed when these propositions were known throughout Germany and within four weeks almost all of Christendom was familiar with them." According to *The Economist*,[2] Luther's first German-language pamphlet "was reprinted 14 times in 1518 alone, in print runs of at least 1,000 copies each time. Of the 6,000 different pamphlets that were published in German-speaking lands between 1520 and 1526, some 1,700 were editions of a few dozen works by Luther. In all, some 6 to 7 million pamphlets were printed in the first decade of the Reformation, more than a quarter of them Luther's." Luther's ideas had gone viral in a pre-digital age.

One can imagine the reaction of the Catholic Church: How dare anyone question the practices of the Church and the authority of the Pope! Who was this upstart? Was he drunk? And: will this simply go away if we ignore it? But the wide dissemination of Luther's comments and ideas meant that the Church would be unable to ignore him. Moreover there was fear that Luther was just the tip of the iceberg and there might be more dissidents; and if enough people realized that others shared their dissatisfaction, the tsunami of religious and social change would be unstoppable. As a result, the Church did what it could to prevent Christian nations

---

[1] Peter Stanford, *Martin Luther, Catholic Dissident* (Hodder & Stoughton 2017), 121.

[2] "How Luther Went Viral", *The Economist* (December 17, 2011): http://www.economist.com/node/21541719.

from being "infected by this ... disorder."[3] Powerful sermons demonized the upstart monk, and his followers were sometimes burned at the stake. Luther himself was excommunicated and often feared for his life.

As we know, the Church failed to crush the Reformation. Once the genie of dissent had been loosed from its bottle, things could never again be the same. The world is now crowded with a number of Christian beliefs and some authors have even suggested that the beginnings of modern capitalism and modern democracy are rooted in new principles and ideas espoused during the Reformation.

Five hundred years on, we see the beginning of a new reformation: a reformation that once again seeks to change the seemingly unchangeable; a reformation that seeks to create a profound and lasting change within a venerable, ancient profession; a reformation that is beginning to reverberate around the globe via a new set of social networks and media.

The Great Legal Reformation.

We live in a time when people of all backgrounds–particularly those without a legal education—are questioning the time-honoured ways of delivering legal services. We live in a time when a traditional, conservative legal profession is increasingly being forced to justify its methods—and perhaps even its existence; a time when dissent against the old order is becoming normalized and circulated globally; a time when newcomers are rewriting the script and challenging the old ways.

The beginning of the Great Legal Reformation lacks the precision of Martin Luther nailing his 95 Theses to the door

---

3   Excerpt from *Edict of Worms* condemning Martin Luther and proclaimed by the Holy Roman Emperor Charles V in 1521.

of the Castle Church, but upheaval in legal services delivery most certainly accelerated and gained strength with the financial crisis of 2008. Since that time, legal regulators, associations, authors, and consulting organizations, from England to Canada to Australia and all parts in between, have prepared numerous books and reports outlining the elements and symptoms of these tumultuous times.[4]

1. A growing body of evidence suggests that demand for legal services from traditional law firms is flattening in several jurisdictions;

2. The "more for less" challenge faced by corporations is a global phenomenon, causing many to: build internal legal teams so as to avoid sending work to law firms, disaggregate legal work among different non-traditional players in the marketplace, and select legal service providers through disciplined procurement processes rather than through personal relationships;

3. Organizations such as Corporate Legal Operations Consortium and Association of Corporate Counsel, share best practices and suggestions among general counsel, chief legal officers and legal operations professionals in order to drive better value and pricing from legal service providers;

4. Global accounting firms are quietly picking away legal work from global law firms;

5. Legal Process Outsourcers (LPO) in countries like South Africa, India, the Philippines, Poland, and Northern Ireland, which have enjoyed chewing

---

[4] See the "Suggested Reading" section at the end of this book.

away at so-called commoditized work for years, are now transitioning to better technology, process, and workflow and continue their climb higher up the legal services food chain;

6. Law schools around the globe continue to pump out thousands of new (and unemployed) graduates each year. Only a small number of institutions, among them Michigan State University Law School, University of Calgary Law School, and the University of Miami's Law Without Walls (to name just a few), are re-thinking legal education to give their graduates skills that go beyond pure legal reasoning;

7. For graduates fortunate enough to be hired as associate lawyers, the traditional partnership model is failing to provide a stable career. Partners are no longer permanent, associates have little chance of becoming partners, and contract lawyers and paralegals continue to replace full-time lawyer hires;

8. Millennials now outnumber the total number of baby boomers, and they also outnumber generation Xers in the workforce. Millennial lawyers come with different attitudes, motivations, and expectations about work. Many of them are not motivated by the lure of partnership 10, 15, or more years down the road. Others aren't motivated by making buckets of money, and most don't see law as a linear career path;

9. Many countries have an ever-widening access-to-justice gap, particularly for those in the middle-class; and

10. Most troubling, lawyers continue to have disproportionately high rates of addiction, depression, anxiety and suicide when compared to the general population.

And if all of that was not enough for a staid, old profession to cope with, the Great Legal Reformation is also sowing the seeds of a technological revolution. The cool kids are "hacking the law" these days: harnessing their collective brainpower to explore new ways of delivering legal services—ways that are better, faster and cheaper. Unconstrained by legacy, image or prestige, the cool kids are excited by the challenge of using technology to break into a centuries-old profession, turning it upside down for the benefit of clients—even lawyers. And while this is not a book about legal technology, it's impossible to ignore; so a short explanation of the current state of legal technology is important to not only understand the risk to legal service providers who fail to harness its power, but also to set the stage for some of the stories in this book.

Technology, and more specifically, legal technology is no longer the sole domain of Silicon Valley nerds; for example, as of June 30, 2017, the website AngelList listed 1,588 legal tech start-ups across the globe with an average valuation of USD$4.2 million. The enthusiasm for change and opportunity is infectious, causing legal tech enthusiasts to gather monthly in an ever-growing number of cities around the world. So much so that one could, if so inclined, overdub the Bowie/Jagger rendition of a hit by Martha and the Vandellas to reflect this global phenomenon:

> *It's an invitation for a revolution, a chance for tech to awe*
> *They'll be laughing and clowning, keyboards pounding,*
> *Hacking on the law,*
> *From Vancouver, BC,*
> *To Santiago, Chile now,*
> *Don't forget them in Nairobi,*
> *Or in the towers of KL,*
> *Back in heat of Sevilla …*

Well, you get the picture.

Every meeting fertilizes new ideas on how to "fix" legal services. And make no mistake, "in need of repair" is very much how the inhabitants of the legal tech world see legal services. They view law as nothing but code and decision-trees (if this, then that), and they pay little heed to tradition. They fearlessly tread where most lawyers dare not, asking questions most lawyers refuse to even contemplate.

Every legal tech gathering I've attended has a similar vibe. There's no tinkering, maybes, or hesitation at them; these events are for believers who want full-bore transformation. The energy is high, the discussions excited and fully engaged. No one questions the premise that technology *will* improve legal service delivery. No one says, "Hang on a moment, law is really complicated—maybe we shouldn't go there." No one asks for permission from the legal establishment or its regulators. Taking their cue from the likes of Uber and Airbnb, the prevailing philosophy is that asking for forgiveness is preferable to seeking permission.

The participants banter around names such as Kira, Beagle, Luminance, Clio, and others as their inspiration. And whether I'm sitting in a brick-and-beam loft space watching computer science engineers drink beer from plastic cups while mingling with young lawyers in jeans, or I'm absorbing the ideas put forth at a loud and brash pitch competition that has more in common with American Idol than Dragon's Den, I'm hard pressed to see how traditional legal services can withstand this onslaught of new ideas.

The journey of ROSS Intelligence, currently one of legal technology's global "darlings" is a great example of what the next decade has in store for the legal profession. In late 2014, the department of computer science at the University of Toronto was invited by IBM to participate in a program that would give students an opportunity to use its artificial intelligence (AI) program, Watson, for any purpose the students determined to be of value. Four computer science students at the University of Toronto were accepted into this new collaboration. IBM placed no real limits on what they could create with Watson; they could use it to solve world hunger, child poverty, climate change, or any societal ill.

Instead, they chose legal services.

One of the team, Jimoh Ovbiagele, remembered how legal bills had financially crippled his single mother when he was growing up. Perhaps, he thought, Watson could help those like his mother afford the legal services they needed. He convinced the rest of the team that legal was the right way to go. After all, Watson was already used in finance and medicine—wouldn't law be the next logical step? The team could see from Jimoh's experience that the delivery system for legal services needed to be fixed. They decided to create a digital legal expert that would assist lawyers and make legal services better, faster, and cheaper.

But the group needed a subject matter expert: someone who could bring a legal background to the project. They found recent University of Saskatchewan law graduate, Andrew Arruda, who was then articling at a Toronto law firm. Arruda would later become Chief Executive Officer of ROSS.

Sometimes dubbed *Siri* for law, ROSS is designed to understand legal questions in regular language—not in key words or complex Boolean searches. For example, a lawyer can ask ROSS the following question: "Can one terminate an employee without notice if she fails to meet her sales target under the employment contract?" ROSS will understand the question and its context, and within a matter of seconds deliver a number of citations and suggested readings so that lawyers get a better picture of the law. The American start-up accelerator, Y Combinator, was the first to invest in ROSS, followed quickly by Dentons Nextlaw project, which made ROSS its very first investment. Now used by a growing number of law firms across the world, ROSS is on track to become one of the top breakthrough technologies in the legal sector. Given the pace at which ROSS has already grown (and ROSS certainly does not own the entire legal AI playing field) it's hard to argue with legal futurist Richard Susskind's assertion that AI will form part of a successful lawyer's toolkit by 2030. In that not-too-distant future, successful law firms will be enterprises staffed by individuals who are fully augmented by technology.

What I find fascinating about the ROSS story is that, despite the University of Toronto being home to an acclaimed Canadian law school, ROSS's initial creation involved none of the law school's faculty or students.

Does that mean that truly innovative solutions to legal services will be found not from within the old order, but from outsiders?

More importantly, why weren't lawyers the ones to create ROSS?

Had lawyers lost sight of the real needs and wants of the marketplace?

How was it that a small group of very young millennials so quickly grasped the potential of AI in legal services and acted upon it, yet an industry filled with thousands of mature, well-educated lawyers, did not?

Legal service incumbents have a great deal of explaining to do.

How long before someone creates a super-expert system that provides specific answers to specific questions (with a stated degree of accuracy) *directly* to clients? In fact, companies like Blue J

Legal,[5] have already created these types of systems for very niche areas of law.

Is it so hard to imagine an online AI system that (with a credit card payment) will answer and provide documentation for the majority of legal problems encountered by everyday people?

As the number of unrepresented people in courtrooms around the world continues to sky-rocket—particularly in matrimonial matters—the answer to better access to justice may, in the words of legal consultant Jordan Furlong, be based "less upon lawyers and more upon alternatives to lawyers."[6] The legal profession's failure to make its services affordable and accessible is not only creating a generation of legal do-it-yourselfers, it's also spawning a generation of legal tech entrepreneurs (nurtured at legal tech incubators like Toronto's Legal Innovation Zone) who are willing to assist them. Many at legal tech gatherings now talk of creating legal chatbots like LawBot and DoNotPay, or of being the next Rocket Lawyer, LegalZoom, Law Scout, Dragon Law or Shake.

How long before the general public begins to view legal services as a technology service that is *merely augmented* by lawyers? Such a suggestion may be heresy for generation Xers and baby boomers. But not so for millennials who have grown up watching technology become the saviour of nearly all things, and who now seek to apply its magic balm to legal services.

---

[5] One of the founders of Blue J Legal is a tax professor at the University of Toronto Law School.

[6] Jordan Furlong, "How Access-to-Justice Efforts Are Changing the Consumer Legal Market," *The Lawyerist* (February 21, 2017): https://lawyerist.com/access-justice-efforts-changing-consumer-legal-market/.

Who knew that technology would bring sexy back to law?

Or maybe millennials have simply run out of the really cool stuff to do and now realize that an entire industry has barely been grazed by technological innovation.

In the face of all this upheaval, how should new or incumbent legal service providers react? Are there already some role models that can lead the way? What would adapting to the Great Legal Reformation entail? Can the traditional business model simply be tweaked or does it require full-scale transformation of systems, pricing, ways of working and career paths? Do some jurisdictions have an advantage over others? Is there a secret sauce to be applied? These were the questions going through my mind from the cozy confines of my home in Toronto.

Many in our digital age, would begin, and end, a search for answers to my questions by scanning the internet. But finding role models and secret sauces is less easy than one would think. If you listen to law firm marketing efforts, hordes of law firms have suddenly become "innovative" and "client-focussed." It seems like barely a month goes by without another firm sending out a press release announcing their latest "innovation partner," or that they've formed an "innovation committee." But how many of these announcements are simply good public relations, and how many are real, actionable, and sustainable? The clatter of information about law firm "innovation" quickly becomes overwhelming, noisy, and confusing. Throw in a pinch of legal innovation failures and this soupy maelstrom makes it easy for the more cynical to dismiss legal innovation at law firms as nothing more than a mirage. Add a dash of exciting new announcements and it's just as easy to swing the masses back to legal innovation nirvana. Just as generals talk about the "fog of war," the "fog of legal innovation" has settled thickly over the legal services industry.[7]

So it's no wonder that Cold War spy George Smiley wrote[8] that a desk is a "dangerous place from which to watch the world," particularly during the Great Legal Reformation. To really understand what's happening at law firms, one needs to get out of the office and poke around in the fog—and so I did.

Unfortunately, what I often found was that whatever innovation exists in most law firms today is incoherent, fragmented, and haphazard—rather than part of a comprehensive strategy to transform in the face of the Great Legal Reformation. Most law firms continue to "muddle through" the Great Legal Reformation in an erratic, undisciplined way without asking the most fundamental questions. Is the current legal services delivery

---

[7] The fog of innovation has even permeated law firms themselves. At the end of 2016, a Law/MBA student at McGill University in Canada, together with a management professor and the Juniper Consulting Group, prepared a small study, *The Illusion of Innovation in Canadian Law Firms.* As the title suggests, they found a huge chasm between the hype of innovation at Canadian law firms and what was actually taking place. For instance, 89 percent of partners surveyed agreed with the statement, "Innovation was one of the firm's highest strategic priorities." In contrast, 58 percent of associates surveyed either disagreed with the statement or were neutral. When asked about innovation leadership, 58 percent of associates felt there was "either no leadership for innovation or no awareness of any innovation leadership at their firm." Meanwhile, 84 percent of partners believed that there was indeed innovation leadership at the firm. Asked if there were incentives to innovate, 59 per cent of associates disagreed, while 33 percent were neutral. Meanwhile, 77 percent of partners and were adamant that such incentives were in place. Most damning was the finding that 70 percent of associates were not aware of any clear channel through which to bring innovative ideas to firm leadership.

[8] John Le Carré, *The Honourable Schoolboy* (Hodder & Stoughton, 1977). See Chapter 4, "The Castle Wakes."

model still fit for purpose in the 21st century? What's the risk of continuing to operate as business as usual? How does a lack of reform affect costs, revenue, clients, and the ability to attract and retain talent? And most importantly, how can we transform in a focused, disciplined way to face the challenges ahead?

But as I waded deeper through the fog of legal innovation, images of some very interesting and unique legal service providers began to sharpen and stand out: providers who actively sought out competitive advantage through the creation of unique client and employee experiences; providers who had made, or were in the process of making, fundamental changes to their business model. And while their approaches vary, they all understand where the Great Legal Reformation is taking the legal services industry and they're willing to move forward with vision, focus, and discipline. What follows are their stories, not only to provide guidance and insight, but also to stir the imagination of a new generation of legal services workers.

PART ONE

THE ENABLING POWER OF
LEGISLATIVE CHANGE

or

HOW I LEARNED TO STOP WORRYING
AND LOVE MY NEW STRUCTURE

CHAPTER 1

SLATER AND GORDON

"Lawyers are Just One Piece of the Puzzle"

For years, I've been interested—my friends would say "obsessed"—with Australia's regulatory regime: one that permits law firms to be owned and operated by persons without legal training. A regime that allows law firms to be publicly traded on the Australian Securities Exchange, giving the average Aussie a piece of the legal meat pie.

To most people, however, such a regulatory environment looks rather mundane and boring. And so my excitement would often be met with blank stares and a patronizing, "Sure, OK mate." But to a multitude of lawyers around the world, the idea of allowing anyone other than lawyers to own or operate a law firm is catastrophic, akin to global nuclear war wrapped up in a super nova.

Not surprisingly then, it was the federal government, not lawyers, that instituted change in Australia; it saw little reason for lawyers to be exempt from competition rules that governed all other Australian businesses. And while the government agreed that lawyer self-regulation was important, self-regulation should not restrict competition unless (i) the objectives of self-regulation *could only* be achieved by restricting competition, and (ii) the benefits of such restrictions outweighed the costs. In short, the legal profession was no longer able to hide behind the facade of self-regulation in order to keep out those without law degrees.

In the mid-1990s, legislative changes were soon enacted across Australian states to allow regular people to own up to 49 percent of a new professional structure called multi-disciplinary practices (MDPs); the new structure also allowed lawyers to mix their practices with those of other professionals, such as accountants. But this was merely a warm-up, as by decade's end another national competition policy review advocated for even further liberalization: that there be no restriction whatsoever on those who could manage or own law firms. Legislators accepted the recommendation and so, on July 1, 2001, New South Wales became the first Australian state, and the first jurisdiction in the world, to allow lawyers to structure themselves as Incorporated Legal Practices (ILPs) without any restriction on share ownership. Other states quickly followed with similar legislation, including the state of Victoria, with its capital city of Melbourne.[9]

Melbourne's Slater and Gordon soon took full advantage of these legislative changes to embark upon the most extreme makeover that any law firm could ever undertake: morphing from a small partnership of seven equity partners into a publicly-traded law corporation in the space of six years.

That firm's journey was the reason for my visit to what's known as the Sports Capital of Australia. My wife and I had arrived in Melbourne two days before and we were staying in a loft-style boutique hotel along Flinders Lane, a location that was

---

[9]   For those interested in a comparative study of the regulation of legal services across English-speaking common law jurisdictions, see Noel Semple, *Legal Services Regulation at the Crossroads: Justitia's Legions* (Edward Elgar Publishing, 2015).

just steps away from a stop for the City Circle Tram that would take me to Slater and Gordon.

The City Circle Tram is a well-preserved antique tram that winds its way through Melbourne's historic city core, lined with magnificent pieces of historic architecture steeped in Victorian grandeur: the Parliament House, the Treasury Building, and the Windsor Hotel; all of which reinforced my preconceived notion of "oldness" that I expected at my 10 a.m. meeting with the Slater and Gordon team. After all, "Slaters," as it's known in Australia, could trace its roots back to the early part of the last century.

As the tram waited for its required jog onto La Trobe Street, I paged through Michael Cannon's book, *That Disreputable Firm ... : the Inside Story of Slater & Gordon*, hoping to get a sense of what I could expect. William, or "Bill," Slater volunteered to join the 10th Australian Field Ambulance during the First World War, then afterwards decided on a career in law. He clerked with Maurice Blackburn (whose firm of the same name remains among Australia's most respected law firms), and after being admitted to practice law in 1922, Bill became partners with Blackburn under the name Blackburn & Slater in Melbourne. Less than a year later, however, Slater struck out on his own and opened his own office in the city on the top floor of Unity Hall.

Soon, however, Slater's love of politics superseded his love of practicing law. In the summer of 1924, the 35-year-old lawyer was chosen as Attorney General for the State of Victoria and for the next eleven years, Slater remained in politics. But in 1935, he decided to revive his old law practice with his brother-in-law, Hugh Lyons Gordon; the new firm would be called Slater and Gordon.

Unfortunately, the partnership was short-lived. Hugh joined the Royal Australian Air Force in 1941 and was killed in action in 1943. Despite Hugh's death, Bill Slater retained the firm name and continued building Slater and Gordon as a personal injury law firm that "assisted the underdog and provided legal services to the disadvantaged" until his death in 1960.

I was reading about the firm's financial difficulties in the mid-1980s—financial difficulties that nearly destroyed it—when the tram started up again and hit the noisy jog in the tracks bringing it onto La Trobe Street. I put my book away and concentrated on the view of the old Courts and caught a brief glimpse of the old Melbourne Gaol where Australia's most famous outlaw, Ned Kelly, was hanged in 1880. Some writers have suggested that poor Ned was an early victim of what we now call the access-to-justice crisis: he couldn't afford an experienced lawyer and had to make do with a cheaper, less experienced one—ultimately to his demise.

At Flagstaff Gardens, I disembarked and walked across the street to a modern, shiny office building that housed the head office of Slater and Gordon, a mere five-minute walk from Unity Hall where Bill Slater had started his practice in the early 1920s. Bill and Hugh likely walked past this site many times, never dreaming that it would one day house Australia's largest consumer law firm, employing over 1,200 people across 54 offices; and another 3,130 people in 27 offices across the United Kingdom.[10] Now Slaters offers much more than personal injury legal services to everyday Australians; its large menu of offerings includes: family law, conveyancing, wills, estate planning and probate, as well as business litigation services, professional negligence

---

[10]   As of December 31, 2016.

litigation, class or group actions, and criminal defence work, among other services.

Entering into Slaters was a far different experience from the one I had imagined while on the tram. Slaters clearly understands the retail legal services sector and has created a separate reception area on the ground floor of its large office building. No need to search a directory, or remember the correct floor; one walks straight in off the street. And there was no shrine to Bill Slater or Hugh Gordon in sight. The reception had a decidedly corporate feel about the place; an entire enterprise was there to assist you, not just a particular person. In fact, clients would be forgiven if they didn't think of "Slaters" as anything more than a generic company name like Google, Apple, or Microsoft.

I had time for only a few sips from my coffee before a helpful gentleman at the reception desk called my name and directed me to the proper elevator and floor.

Game on, I thought.

Time to see what this puppy was all about.

A New Era Needs a New Structure

During the short ride up the elevator, I began thinking about the traditional structure of law firms and how law schools spend no time teaching law students how to structure and properly manage their firms; as a result, lawyers simply default to creating a partnership (or, where allowed, a wholly-owned personal corporation) and muddle along. Of course, firms of even a modest size require a specific lawyer to manage the thing; that someone is either elected, or shanghaied, into becoming the firm's managing partner.

Along with being the face of the firm, the managing partner takes responsibility for strategy, risk management, tactics, and administration of law firm operations—all while managing her own law practice. The luckier ones will have their practices looked after by other lawyers while in management.

Behemoth firms with hundreds of lawyers are typically run by a managing partner, who has the advice and support of an executive council, all of whom will also be lawyers and partners in the firm. They are, to think of it another way, a set of elite lawyers who govern the firm's operations–sometimes known by the most cynical as a Star Chamber. Many large law firms will employ the services of a CEO and even a CFO (neither of whom is a lawyer) to assist with day-to-day operations. However, despite the lofty titles, these roles lack the authority, power, and importance that they have in a non-legal business corporation.

More often than not, the business experience of the managing partner and any executive council is limited to their experience within the law firm itself. Depending on the size of the partnership, all partners will vote on most decisions proposed by the managing partner. It's a chaotic, politically-motivated decision-making process sometimes referred to by realists as "herding cats"—I apologize to cats for the comparison. To address the defects in this decision-making process, partners of large firms will cede a large amount of authority to the managing partner and to her executive council, allowing them to make all but the most major decisions on their behalf. As one managing partner once told me, "we're a partnership, but we run our firm like a corporation." I wanted to ask if he advises his business clients to structure and operate in a similar fashion, but I was unnaturally polite that day.

The partnership structure served Slaters fairly well throughout the 20th century. However, by the turn of the century, a majority

First Contact

Despite its many accessible locations, most clients start their Slaters experience with a phone call. They have a legal problem, they pick up the phone and call a central 1-800-number. They may have seen a Slaters TV commercial or one of its other ad campaigns that drive nearly 80,000 enquiries each year in Australia alone—all handled by specially-trained staff centralized at its Melbourne base.

Formal legal training is not a requirement to work at Slaters' call centre, but staff are trained to understand the different areas of law Slaters offers and to triage calls using workflows built to deal with every aspect of a call. The call centre team asks the right questions, understands the issues, and makes the initial determination of whether or not the client's legal needs are ones for which Slaters can offer assistance. And make no mistake, Slaters is particular about the type of client it acts for—a proportion of enquires are screened out and referred to other more appropriate providers.

Many law students begin their legal careers in the Slaters call centre, hoping they'll be hired on as lawyers after passing their admission exams. Others choose a Slaters career path that begins at the call centre, moves to lead a team in the call centre, then perhaps shifts to become a project manager in change management, or to a role in data analytics, all without ever practicing law.

The call centre is also a data-rich environment. If a minimum number of calls are not being directed to certain offices, Slaters will consider ramping up a local marketing campaign to drive more calls to those offices. Data analytics are an important part of the firm's competitive advantage and the number of enquiries given to each lawyer from the call centre (and the number converted to clients) are tracked. Slaters understands where clients and potential clients are clustered by postal code and intimately understands its clients so as to take advantage of cross-selling opportunities that arise due to demographics, life stage and geography. Diligently tracking data allows Slaters to have a firm grasp on where files are coming from and therefore what resourcing needs to be put into place to reduce wait times and provide quality client service. Data analytics also allow Slaters to match lawyers with offices closer to their homes in order to provide better work/life balance—or to shift people to offices with increased demand. Much like retail banking, some of the most progressive career opportunities at Slaters are in its suburban offices.

of Slaters' partners determined that in order to stay true to the firm's mission of providing accessible legal services to everyday Australians, the firm needed to offer a more diverse range of legal advice, and that wider range of advice had to be based on a national platform. However, the firm's partnership structure at the time would not allow that vision to become reality. Slaters not only needed access to a greater pool of capital to invest heavily in IT infrastructure, team careers, and in direct-to-consumer marketing, it also needed access to a wider pool of business expertise and experience.

In 2001 Slaters converted from a partnership to an ILP, then listed on the Australian Securities Exchange in 2007. The few Slaters partners who voted against such a transformation were moved on. Since Slaters went public in 2007, only a very few other legal services offerings have listed on the Australian Securities Exchange, with varying degrees of success.

Andrew Grech, whom I would meet later, was the founding managing director (and a director on Slaters' board of directors) of the publically-floated Slater and Gordon. And while Slaters' management team was comprised of some of his former partners, they were fully accountable to an independent board of directors selected by skill-set: people with deep experience in risk management, capital markets, retail, governance, human relations, and technology, to name just a few. This outside experience is powerful and vital to Slaters' future, Andrew Grech later told me. "We need different, independent thinkers on our board. It helps us avoid a myopic view of the world." Slaters' board composition is also designed to send a strong signal on gender diversity; 50 percent of the board is to be populated by female directors and Slaters' first board chair was a woman.

Technology + Workflow + People

Upon arrival, the elevator doors opened to a classic office layout with a reception desk and a suite of conference rooms. The receptionist ushered me into the conference room that I would call home during my time there and offered me a selection of beverages. Nothing distinguished this area of the firm from that of any other large law firm I had ever visited. The area was modern and well laid out, but not overly so. This was clearly not where Slaters was investing the bulk of its money.

Reminiscent of retail business strategies employed by many successful global companies, Slaters makes considerable investments in IT infrastructure and business processes. "We focus first on creating the best business process and workflow," Jonathan Pangrazio, group head of IT, told me via a rather terrible phone connection. He wasn't in Melbourne at the time of my visit and so we resorted to a bad combination of hands-free cellular phone service and office speaker phone. "We then build IT around that process. Our goal is to be the most technologically-enabled legal services business in the world."

As our conversation continued, I had to pinch myself several times to ensure that I was hearing things correctly. We talked at length about the importance of process and technology as the cornerstones of Slaters' competitive advantage: the way Slaters sets itself apart from its competitors. It was distinctly different from the conversations I've had with traditional law firms, which always start with, "Our lawyers are really great" and always ends with, "Our lawyers are really great." However, there were still more conversations to be had and I was sure that stories of the excellent abilities of Slaters' lawyers would soon reveal themselves.

Unfortunately, I was also stuck with my speaker phone for my chat with Ken Fowlie, who was then CEO of Slaters Australia. The connection was much better, but like my conversation with Jonathan, it was less and less about lawyers. In fact, Ken proudly told me that because of Slaters' reputation for opportunity and openness to new ideas, the firm was facing a situation virtually unknown to traditional law firms: job applicants from a broad cross-section of industries—all with no law firm experience. The firm had actually done the impossible, become an enticing place to work for those without a law degree.

"Our pool of candidates is broader and deeper than it's ever been," he told me. "We're able to attract people with terrific experience, who previously would never have thought of working at a law firm. When you realize that legal services is miles behind where other service industries are now, and we can bring in people who have gone through similar changes in those industries, such as banking, financing, insurance, or telecommunications, there's a lot we can learn from them. The experience and insight from other consumer-facing industries is invaluable."

But where would all these non-legally trained people fit in? Isn't the engine of growth for law firms the lawyers themselves? Isn't that where scale is achieved? It seemed odd that a law firm would be looking for more than technical experts in the law.

Ken's voice crackled over the speaker phone. "It's critical for us to implement a business-process approach, and we've seen the importance of having dedicated resources in areas such as business process, business process improvement, and business analysis. The best people are those who understand legal services but aren't captured by the current process—they have greater understanding of how those processes can be improved."

"We have a good footprint in Australia," Ken continued. "And an ongoing challenge for us is how to configure it to best serve our clients. Being local is very important to our clients; we can't compromise that. But we need to consider new ways to transact work and deliver that work to our clients as we build scale. It's often through achieving scale that we can be more creative in tackling some of these challenges."

Again, I heard nothing about the greatness of Slaters' lawyers.

"Everyone here has a role to play in delivering quality legal services," Ken told me, perhaps sensing my confusion over the phone. "Every interaction with the client is critically important and there are lots of ways to mess it up. So all points of contact are important."

Slaters' clients are, like most non-corporate consumers of legal services, fairly price sensitive. This forces the firm to constantly improve how it manages labour costs and staffing mixes. So it's little wonder that the firm places a great deal of importance on team members who didn't graduate from law school. Underpinning it all is a focus on learning and development that encourages employees to build competencies and to become more autonomous, all supported by appropriate workflow. Slaters goes to great lengths to skill up clerks and non-legally trained staff with the right supervision and the right workflow to enhance the client experience and, at the same time, create opportunities for its teams. The firm is willing to constantly experiment with different team compositions and workflow to ensure maximum efficiency and client satisfaction for each area of law.

In the Superannuation department for example, files were originally sent to a team that included a lawyer and several clerks, with many of the tasks within each file divided among the clerks. Some did forms, some saw clients—but no one had total ownership over the file as a whole, while the lawyer struggled to manage the whole thing. The revised process now gives each clerk 100 files and a budget. All initial claims are handled by clerk teams, and it's only if a claim receives an initial rejection from government authorities that it moves to a lawyer.

As one practice group leader later told me, "Lawyers are just one piece of the puzzle here, whereas at other firms, lawyers are the entire puzzle. That informs so many levels of what we do and how the lawyer and assistant act. Our legal assistants share ownership of files. And that kind of empowerment makes everyone feel greater than themselves."

Measuring

Much of the work done for Slaters' clients is based on fixed fees or on some sort of contingency arrangement—after all, Slaters pioneered "no win, no fee" in Australia in the 1980s. These types of fee arrangements present problems for conventional law firms that measure performance based on the number of hours billed by a particular lawyer. In traditional law firms, the more hours an associate or employee or partner bills, the better her performance is deemed to be. These firms use "time spent" as a simplistic, but important, key performance indicator. It also means these firms place more value on the time taken to deliver legal services than on the output actually achieved.

Slaters takes a different view.

The firm starts with what's important for the success of its clients, then combines that with items aligned with its strategic vision, firm culture, and the long-term sustainability of the firm to develop relevant key performance indicators. Lawyers are advanced, and rewarded, using a "balanced scorecard" approach: a combination of financial performance (the firm's and the lawyer's); contributions made to brand and marketability; contributions to nurturing and developing others within the firm; contributions to the intellectual capacity of the firm (knowledge management contributions); the ability of lawyers to convert enquiries triaged from the call centre into clients; the length of time it takes to move files from one stage to the next; budget management; and so on.

Slaters also conducts spot audits on its lawyers—currently 98 percent of its lawyers are audited for the purpose of practice improvement. The audits are done internally, not through an outside provider, and lawyers are given a map of issues found, as well as guidance and assistance to improve. Lawyers are held accountable for improvement, but not in an oppressive way. These audits are also a two-way street as they allow lawyers to make suggestions on how to improve firm standards as well their own personal standard.

Career Paths for Lawyers

I wondered about the lawyer career path. Was it the traditional ridiculous duel to the death which has been aptly named, the "tournament"[11]—a gladiatorial forum pitting associate against associate, and friend against friend, destroying any sense of collegiality as lawyers fight to grasp the brass ring of partnership? Even US Navy SEALS, I thought, work together as a team

---

[11] The term "tournament" was first coined by Galanter and Palay to explain the ruthless, inefficient, and absurd career progression from associate to partner in big law firms. See: Marc Galanter and Thomas Palay, "Why the Big Get Bigger: The Promotion to Partner Tournament and the Growth of Large Law Firms," *Virginia Law Review*, 76, no. 4 (1990): 747-811.

throughout their brutal culling-out process. Not so in traditional law firms.

Unsurprisingly, Slaters takes a different approach.

Lawyers can, if they choose, move along a more traditional path of associate to senior associate. With seniority comes encouragement to take leadership roles in areas of practice, or within geographic locations. Slaters encourages team members to look where opportunities exist and see them as opportunities for their own careers. Never was that more apparent than when I met Dina Tutungi. Pleasant and energetic—like all the Slaters' personnel I met—her drive and youthful appearance belied the fact that she had already garnered many years of experience as a lawyer.

Dina started at Slaters in 2001 as a junior lawyer, fresh out of law school and ready to fight for her clients' rights. But she also came from a small-business family, so it wasn't long before she began to see new business opportunities for Slaters, her practice area, and for herself.

"By 2006 I could see that we were receiving an increasing number of clients and enquiries from Ringwood," Dina said, referring to a suburb of Melbourne. "I also noticed that our competitors were beginning to open offices in Ringwood. I knew that Slaters should be there as well." The passion in her voice was obvious.

"I spoke to Andrew Grech, provided him with my business plan, and he said 'go for it!' How many firms would allow a fifth-year lawyer to open up a new office?"

"None that I know of," I replied, trying to suppress my utter amazement.

"The trust put in me by management was key—it's hard to get these kinds of opportunities elsewhere."

As I was processing what she'd just said, Dina added, "It's part of our culture to give people opportunities—it's normal. I've moved around a lot—there always seems to be opportunities to do something new and different here. It's incredible."

Dina later returned to the Melbourne office where she rose through a number of managerial roles to where, at the time of writing, she is now general manager of personal injury law Victoria and a member of the national executive. But I was most interested in her stint as national practice group leader of superannuation claims, total & permanent disability claims, where her group became one of the fastest growing practices at the firm simply by implementing a minor twist to the client intake process. "I was able to make it compulsory for all offices and all persons who open files, to ask every client very specific questions about possible superannuation claims," she told me. "We were also able to monitor referral rates by office, and by lawyer, to ensure that our clients were well looked after in this area." This was cross-selling legal services on steroids, I thought. Every firm talks about the importance of cross-selling and how it's always easier to get work from existing client than to get new clients—but I had never seen anything as simple and elegant as what Dina had implemented to achieve that goal.

Dina also created an online tool for clients to determine if they had a superannuation claim by answering a series of simple questions. If the likelihood of a claim was high, the online tool would generate a referral to the appropriate Slaters' team member for follow-up, and information from that questionnaire would prepopulate the file if the firm was retained.

As I calculated the hours needed for all Dina's achievements, she casually wondered how much longer the interview would take as it was close to 4 p.m. and she needed to pick up her daughter.

Of course she did.

Dina, like other Slaters' personnel, had been working part-time for several years. "The women working here are very happy," she said. "There's still work to be done. Nothing is perfect but the starting point is this: if someone is going on parental leave, the expectation is that they're going to return part-time, so how do we do that? And the same rules apply for men."

Her comments supported the Slaters' philosophy, which was shared with me throughout my discussions there. I had heard several times: "We don't churn through lawyers," and, "We prefer to elongate the careers of lawyers we've invested in." It was a refreshing change to the dog-eat-dog mentality I was so used to seeing in law firms.

Growth by Acquisition

In the early years, Slaters went on a spree in the marketplace, picking up a large number of smaller firms to quickly build its national platform. At the same time, legislative changes had begun to limit compensation in some practice areas, and the only way to continue to provide that type of legal service was by becoming bigger, so it wasn't unusual for firms to approach Slaters to purchase them, many of which saw Slaters as their exit strategy.

And so far, at least in Australia, Slaters seems to have mostly gotten it right in terms of the firms it has acquired, retaining large proportions of the lawyers and employees of these firms.

For these acquisitions as well as for lateral hires, Slaters spent a great deal of time on "fit," determining if the new lawyers could deal with the challenges of change and improvement—as well as ensuring that the lawyers' values aligned with those of Slaters. "You've got to come with a willingness to adapt," one senior Slaters executive told me. "Otherwise this can be a difficult place."

Lawyers, however, are not known for their willingness and ability to adapt, so eventually Slaters preferred organic growth in

Australia with an "internal first" policy for new roles; such organic growth is also seen as a good way to extend the career horizons and capabilities of people already in the organization.

"We're on a journey," another senior Slaters executive told me. "We haven't got it all figured out. So far we've been able to draw people along the pathway, and harness their ideas, energy and enthusiasm. We're still transforming and we're closer to the beginning than to the end."

Leadership

Eventually, it came time for my meeting with Slaters' then managing director. Andrew Grech had joined Slaters in 1994 as a personal injury lawyer, then became the firm's managing director in 2000, and steered the firm through its great transformation.

I had imagined that Andrew Grech would be a larger-than-life archetypal CEO with an intimidating stare, and an arrogant matter-of-fact way of speaking. Someone with unbridled ambition and a massive ego that demanded constant feeding. The kind of person that commands respect, but whom you would never invite over for dinner. I had met many of those types running law firms around the world. So when a quiet, bespectacled gentlemen entered the small boardroom, saying, "Hello Mitch, can I get you a coffee? Tea? Water?" I naturally assumed that Andrew was running late and that this pleasant guy was just helping me kill some time until he was available. However, this *was* Andrew Grech: more like the kind of guy you could easily strike up a chat with at a pub than the power-wielding CEO of my imagination.

I asked him about his transition from personal injury lawyer to a pure business role at Slaters. "All people go through stages in their life," Andrew said. "I got into law, and particularly personal injury law, because I wanted to help people. That's the entry point. How can I solve this seemingly complex and insolvable problem for my clients? The intellectual satisfaction from that pushed me onward."

"And now?" I asked.

"Now, God forbid that they should let me get near a client—for the client's sake!" He laughed. Unlike managing partners at many firms, Andrew was never going to practice law again. No one was looking after a practice for him while he dabbled with managing the firm for a few years. He was fully and totally committed to a permanent career change. And despite the fact that Andrew could have sprinkled our conversation with thinly veiled boasts, he didn't. "My primary purpose," he said, "is determining how we can make the law more accessible to our clients. How do we use capital as a tool to make the law more accessible to ordinary people? And how can I provide our team with the tools they need to excel—capital, information management systems, marketing and business development systems—and to provide an exceptional client experience?" This guy was a true believer in the firm's vision. More importantly, he believed that the vision was much bigger than himself. To have a leader who sees himself as existing to serve the enterprise, rather than the other way around, was refreshing. "The reason why our lawyers can be efficient and effective," he continued, "is because of the machinery sitting underneath them. All they have to focus on is being good lawyers. We've built an infrastructure that allows us to go for gold and that's exciting."

Unlike a partnership in which the most powerful partners are able to move the firm in a certain direction regardless of the long-term consequences, Andrew has no such power over Slaters' board of directors; he holds only one vote. "It's refreshing to have the intellectual honesty of an independent board," he told me. "I have to make my case like everyone else." He also made it clear to me that he didn't miss the days of partnership with its "swagger and ego. We have no rock stars here who can hold you over a barrel," and the firm isn't beholden to one or a small number of clients. "As a result, we have very little key client risk and very little key lawyer risk."

Slaters' corporate structure also has the added benefit of creating greater separation between the interests of the business, and the personal interests and careers of employees. "In a partnership, partners often see the world only through the lens of their own personal interests," Andrew told me. "As a result, their decision-making is often coloured by personal interests. Operating as a corporation makes an enormous difference to our culture. It's much easier to embed values in a corporate environment than in a partnership which many lawyers see as nothing more than a cooperative venture where office expenses and staff are shared." Breaking the "what's in it for me?" mindset was critical to developing Slaters as a true legal services enterprise committed to a long-term vision. Separating the best interests of the business from the best interests of individual careers, "combined with the idea that while everyone is important, no one is *that* important, is fundamental to how we think," Andrew continued. "It's how we support each other's careers and the way we build opportunity for one another." It also contributes to a unique set of values and the firm culture.

"The more we talk about values as an organization, the more we find ourselves having that conversation with our teams, and as a result, the more embedded and more valued those principles become, and the more those principles translate into behaviours." However, Andrew was quick to point out that Slaters' values are works-in-progress that need to be continually refreshed and tested to determine their relevancy and their resonance with teams and clients: are employees living those values and are those values affecting behaviour? "Exceptional performance," he said, "is

Our Mission

To give people easier access to world class legal services.

Our Values

1. Do It Right

☐ I aim to always exceed my client's expectations
☐ I always endeavour to act with the highest professional standards
☐ I deliver what I promise
☐ I make informed decisions using quality information
☐ I communicate openly, honestly, clearly and constructively
☐ I demonstrate my passion for what S&G is trying to achieve by my work
☐ I am thoughtful about how I use resources

2. Work Well With Others

☐ I work with, trust and support others
☐ I encourage, respect and recognise the contributions that others make
☐ I share knowledge, experience and ideas
☐ I connect clients, colleagues and the community
☐ I empathise with others and value individual differences
☐ I contribute to an enjoyable workplace

3. Take The Lead

☐ I am committed to doing all I can to help my clients achieve their goals
☐ I strive to be the best I can be
☐ I take initiative and ownership for finding better ways of doing things
☐ I take accountability for my actions
☐ I adapt to and embrace change

*Source: Slater and Gordon intranet

driven by people understanding purpose, and feeling they have sufficient autonomy to influence that purpose—and to influence their ability to achieve that purpose."

I had to ask him a question that has sparked discussion among lawyers worldwide. What about the risk that unethical behaviour will occur in the corporate environment, given that lawyers are no longer controlling the entity?

Andrew paused before answering. "Partnership as an organizing model is no guarantee of ethical behaviour, as evidenced by some of the great ethical lapses by law firms over the years. I'm not sure that the defining difference in determining behaviour norms is correlated to any organizational structure to any large degree. Having said that, in my experience, a corporatized structure with external shareholders has a greater focus on governance, and a strong economic imperative to maintain reputation— so evidence and common sense suggests that such a structure should lead to higher standards. We also find that our more conventional management structure delivers better outcomes than in a partnership model."

"And those pesky questions about conflicts of interest?" I asked.

In its corporate governance policy, he explained, Slaters has set out that it "has a primary duty to the Court, as well as duties to its clients. If there is an inconsistency or conflict between the duties to the court, to clients and to shareholders then that conflict or inconsistency is resolved as follows: (1) the duty to the Court will prevail over all duties; and (2) the duty to the client will prevail over the duty to shareholders."

Many lawyers, I suggested to him, find the way Slaters does business to be distasteful; they feel that Slaters is commoditizing law and ruining the profession; that law should not just be another business. Andrew minced few words in response. "Look, a professional is someone who applies their intelligence and skills in order to provide a service in a way that is accessible to clients—so that clients can use it. Part of accessibility is affordability. My job is to ensure that everyday people have access to world-class legal services in a way that is accessible to them—which includes affordability. The primary thing is the client, and the role of lawyers in preserving the administration of justice. Tradition is secondary."

Epilogue

No discussion of Slaters would be complete without mention of its disastrous £675 million acquisition of the professional services division of Quindell PLC in 2015. Based in the UK, this division was made up of several components complementary to personal injury services: the costs firm Compass Law; the law firms of Pinto Potts, Silverbeck Rymer, and The Compensation Lawyers; as well as marketing, health, and motor vehicle services. The acquisition instantly doubled Slaters UK headcount and gave Slaters just over 10 percent market share of the UK personal injury market—more than double that of its closest rivals. On its face, the acquisition seemed to be a "transformational opportunity."

Soon, however, this transformational opportunity became the stuff of Greek tragedy. Shortly after the May 2015 closing of this acquisition, Quindell (which later changed its name to Watchstone Group) announced that it was being investigated by the UK's Serious Fraud Office over its past accounting practices, triggering concerns that Slaters had overpaid for the assets it had just purchased. In November 2015, the UK government also announced plans to institute new limits and procedures for certain personal injury claims, plans which negatively impacted Slaters' future UK revenues from personal injury services.

Then things got even worse.

Also in late 2015, Slaters adopted a new accounting standard for work-in-progress, which, in addition to an AUS$814.2 million impairment in goodwill from the Quindell acquisition, triggered massive write-downs and as a result, large losses. The Australian Securities and Investment Commission began an investigation into the accuracy of Slaters' financial accounts and records—one that later found no wrongdoing. Slaters' share price tanked and two shareholders' class actions were commenced in 2016—one of which was steered by Maurice Blackburn, the firm that had once embraced Bill Slater as a partner nearly 100 years before.

In spring 2017, Slaters' debt (which was now huge) was sold off by its Australian bankers to American companies specializing in acquiring distressed debt. Rated by some analysts as a "sell" in early 2017, Slaters had written off over 60 percent of the Quindell purchase price by the end of April 2017, and its shares then languished around $0.10 per share, down from $8.07 when the Quindell deal was completed only 24 months before. In June 2017, Slaters served and filed a lawsuit against Watchstone Group for approximately £600 million. This lawsuit, even if successful, will do little to take the sting out of Slaters' troubles. The paper fortunes of Andrew Grech, Ken Fowlie (who took over UK operations), and other Slaters employees have evaporated.

In early June, 2017, yet another shareholder class action was threatened against Slaters, but at the time of writing had not yet been filed and served. Andrew Grech resigned as managing director in late June 2017, in advance of a debt-for-equity swap scheduled to close in October 2017; the swap would give Slaters' debt holders at least 95 percent of the firm's shares, significantly diluting all other shareholders. In conjunction with this debt-to-equity swap, the class action steered by Maurice Blackburn, was "settled in principle" in July, 2017 for AUD$36.5 million.

Yet, despite the storm, Slaters is still operating. Traditional law firms have very low stress tolerance and often break apart, even when profitable (just not profitable enough for the partners). Time and again it has been shown that partners at traditional firms are more loyal to themselves than to their firms, making these entities exceptionally fragile. If Slaters had been a traditional law firm partnership, it would have dissolved long before now, leaving its employees and clients in the lurch. Slaters' transformation into a true legal enterprise is the only reason why it remains in operation. Slaters created an entity-driven delivery model where legal acumen was important, but it was only table stakes; it was a given and it was expected. It's why my discussions at Slaters didn't centre on the quality of their lawyers (and yes, Slaters does have great lawyers), but rather on how to harness that quality and deliver it in a cost-effective and accessible way to those who need it. Slaters' secret sauce (technology, workflow, process, culture) could not move to other law firms on a whim; these things remained in place, creating value for clients, employees, and yes, even shareholders. The secret sauce enabled Slaters to survive a situation that would have very quickly destroyed a traditional law firm.

Slaters' near-death experience has delighted many lawyers who now fall all over themselves to be the first to claim, "I told you so. A floated law firm should never have been permitted." This is complete and utter nonsense, and it conveniently ignores the true reason behind Slaters' troubles: a single business decision that turned out to be catastrophic. Becoming publicly traded allowed Slaters to invest in better technology; take a balanced scorecard approach to career advancement; move away from the billable hour; create a collaborative approach to law with better processes; skill up employees and seek new opportunities for them; separate the interests of the business from the interests of the lawyers; refuse to churn through lawyers; and create better governance with wider, more diverse business expertise. All of which ensured its long-term survival in the face of the harshest circumstances. Slaters' troubles did not stem from any professional negligence on its part, nor from an ethical lapse or conflict of interest. There's also no evidence of structural or operational defects. But for the Quindell acquisition, it's unlikely that Slaters would be facing the hurricane of negative headlines, lawsuits, and debt restructuring.

Slaters found competitive advantage in being an efficient, data- and tech-driven business with scale which allowed the firm to compete in highly price-sensitive areas of law. It made focussed investments in technology, process, and workflow to optimize work allocation across geography and personnel. Slaters' sophisticated management and corporate governance structure ensured that its culture, values, investment, compensation, and career development all aligned with its strategy—and put the long-term interests of the firm ahead of any short-term individual interests.

No matter the final outcome, Slaters' structure, operations, strategy, and vision remain sound, and worthy of study by legal service providers that wish to thrive in the Great Legal Reformation.

CHAPTER 2
THE SALVOS

" ...men and women, weary and worn in the battles of life, need someone to whom they can go when pressed down ..."

Slaters is not the only law firm in Australia to structure itself as an ILP and allow those dastardly "non-lawyers" to take a piece of the action or manage law firms. But despite Australia's growing legion of over 71,000 lawyers, there seem to be fewer than 6,000 ILPs[12] spread across that sun-baked continent. Many ILPs are small firms that use the structure to give employees a stake in the practice, create retirement annuities for shareholders, incent good governance, and provide better access to management expertise. For such firms, the ability to raise capital is not the prime motive to create ILP, although having that flexibility is an added bonus.

"Flexibility" was the key, I thought while sitting for breakfast with my wife in a small café on the ground floor of Sydney's historic shopping paradise, the Queen Victoria Building. It wasn't that the form of a law firm was good or bad, but whether or not that form allowed for the greatest creativity of purpose. It wasn't that regulations should just drive good behaviour; they must

---

[12]   Based on numbers provided by law societies in Victoria (1,576), New South Wales (2,027) and South Australia (232). The number of ILPs in Queensland, Northern Territory and Western Australia were unavailable and were estimated by the author. Tasmania has 125 ILPs.

also refrain from stifling ideas that their drafters had not even contemplated.

"Don't you feel like we're tilting," my wife said suddenly, breaking me from my thoughts.

"What do you mean?"

"Tilting. The floor has a definite slope to it."

I looked at the exquisitely tiled floor, comparing it to the shop windows. She was right! The floor sloped eastward—back toward the small art deco hotel on Castlereagh Street where we were staying. As it turns out, the slope is deliberate and follows the land upon which it's built. And that slope not only leads to our hotel, but also to another creative product spawned by Australia's decision to loosen restrictions on law firm ownership. A product that is among the most exciting around the globe.

Many large firm lawyers complain of a lack of purpose: that they've become so consumed with the day-to-day focus of making monthly billing targets that they've lost sight of why they went to law school. Idealism dashed, and without answers to the question "what's it all about," many switch their purpose to a lifetime of chasing higher billing in order to support a lifestyle they never knew they needed—until they obtained it. Alienation from initial dreams can be a fertile ground for depression, alcoholism, and other addictions: social problems that run in extremely high numbers among lawyers.

Millennials appear to be the cohort most likely to rebel against such alienation. A great deal is written about millennials, what they want, how they're to be managed and what excites them. But a common thread seems to be that millennials are most likely to believe that *purpose* is equal in importance to *profit,* and that there should be a way for the two to peacefully co-exist in any enterprise. It's not that millennials believe that profit is bad, but rather, that profit in and of itself is not particularly purposeful—and as a result, being part of a profitable enterprise, without a clear mission or clear purpose, is not a long-term motivator for this generation. So is it any surprise that a purposeful law firm would hatch from the mind of a millennial?

Salvos Legal Humanitarian and its sister entity, Salvos Legal Limited, sit on the second floor of an unremarkable office building along Castlereagh Street, mere steps from my hotel. Their existence is owed solely to one of those mundane life events that only in hindsight can be seen as an alignment of the stars.

In 2003, 22-year-old newly-minted lawyer Luke Geary agreed to a pleasant dinner-in with his flatmate and two of the flatmate's friends. These friends were highly involved in the Salvation Army (or "the Salvos" as it's referred to in Australia) in Auburn, a highly diverse but rough suburb west of Sydney, which also acts as one of Australia's largest catch basins for new immigrants. Perhaps the dinner was a set-up all along, or perhaps it was truly happenstance, but upon hearing that Luke was a lawyer, the Salvos friends launched into the story of an elderly woman in Auburn who was about to lose custody of her three small grandchildren; their mother was a heroin addict and their father, a violent alcoholic. The grandmother had been the primary caregiver—and a very good one—for these children, but Community Services had now come to the conclusion that she was no longer fit to care for them.

There are many responses that Luke could have made that evening. He could have made unkind comments about the parents. He could have shaken his head at the tragedy and lamented the injustice. He might even have offered to donate some money to the Salvos and changed the subject to rugby.

Luke took a different and life-changing tack—not only for this family, but for himself and the entire state of New South Wales.

"How can I help?" he asked before adding, "Although you should know that I don't do that kind of law." At the time, Luke specialized in commercial litigation for large corporations and had just joined a mid-sized Sydney law firm that focussed on commercial law.

"Well," said one of the Salvos friends, trying unsuccessfully to suppress his obvious joy, "She has no one else to turn to, so you'll be better than nothing!"

Soon Luke was digging into the file—and wondering what he had got himself into. But, much like Slaters' Andrew Grech, his desire to help, coupled with the challenge of solving a seemingly complex and unsolvable problem, pushed him onward. Fighting Community Services in the Children's Court would be a daunting task on any occasion, but this case also involved three other lawyers who were acting for the government, the children's designated representative, and the father: all of whom opposed Luke's client's desire to care for the children. Despite the legal firepower brought to bear against him, Luke was able to convince the court that the bases upon which the opposing parties were purporting to remove the children were unsupported by any facts. The grandmother was awarded full custody.

The Salvos was understandably ecstatic!

"They asked me to come to the Salvation Army in Auburn one Sunday," Luke told me, sitting back in his chair. He adjusted his dark, square, yet stylish, glasses. His short hair, clean-shaven face and intense demeanour all screamed "big city lawyer." The kind of guy who would not be mistaken for anyone *but* a lawyer— perhaps even without his suit on. Some people just have "the look." Perhaps that's why his clients feel comforted and supported by him—they have their own big legal gun standing by their side.

"They wanted to thank me in person for taking the case on. I had some trepidation as I had heard of the uniforms and," he smiled, "the tambourines." Other than for this case, Luke's contact with the Salvos had been limited to seeing uniformed members collecting donations for the needy at train stations. "It all went well. However, before I left someone else asked me to take on another case. And so I did that case and was asked to come back to be thanked a second time. And when I came back, I was again asked to take on another case."

"They knew a good thing when they saw one," I said.

He laughed. "And then it happened once more after that! They're a very impressive group—ninety percent are volunteering somewhere in the community. It soon became my church."

Two years and dozens of cases later, Luke took what he shyly referred to as his "hobby" to the next level. He set up a free legal clinic in an outdoor courtyard adjacent to the church, and called the clinic Courtyard Legal. Courtyard Legal soon became a significant legal practice growing to over 750 cases, all while Luke was working full time.

By 2009 he was running out of spare time to manage his "hobby." In addition, he had also moved his litigation practice to Mills Oakley, a large Sydney law firm that could trace its roots back to 1864: a firm that now wanted the rising star to become a partner. Hard decisions would have to be made—and soon. The lure of prestige and big money as a partner at a respected Sydney law firm was a temptation not to be resisted by many. Nonetheless, in what was surely seen by his colleagues as a fit of madness, Luke left Mills Oakley shortly after becoming a partner—but not without a plan.

The Salvos loved what Luke had created at Courtyard Legal; they didn't want to lose it. The Salvos offered him the opportunity to run Courtyard Legal on a full-time basis as a paid employee. Luke agreed, but on condition that he could build Courtyard

Legal into something much bigger, something that would be self-supporting.

"I told the Salvos that if this is to work, we need to ensure it's self-funding, and that, to the extent we can, the lawyers involved needed to be paid. We can't rely upon volunteers for everything." And while the Salvos might be able to afford to finance such a project itself, it would be a serious drain on its resources.

So how to do it in a way that made financial sense?

Early in 2010, Luke was hired as the first general counsel of the Salvos–a role that had three key components: (1) continue to run Courtyard Legal; (2) create a new, financially sensible business model; and (3) recruit the appropriate teams.

Less than a year later, on November 1, 2010, two new legal entities made a splash in the Australian legal marketplace: Salvos Legal Limited and Salvos Legal Humanitarian Limited. As James Condon, Commissioner of the Salvos, told Australian television news station, ABC, "It's the most exciting new initiative [of the] Salvation Army in Australia in 130 years."[13]

James Condon had every right to be excited. "Neither of these entities receives any government funding, nor do they receive funding from the Salvos," Luke told me. "We're completely self-sustaining." The secret sauce to this structure comes from the same Australian regulatory regime that allowed Slaters to grow: unrestricted management and ownership of law firms. Salvos Legal Limited and Salvos Legal Humanitarian Limited are both ILPs that are wholly-owned by the Salvos. In addition, there

---

[13] James Condon, interviewed by Rebecca Baillie on Australian Broadcasting Corporation News (July 28, 2011): http://www.abc.net.au/7.30/content/2011/s3280519.htm.

are four directors for each company, 75 percent of whom are appointed by the Salvos and must be trustees of the Salvos.

Control by the Salvos was critical. "It prevents mission creep," Luke said. "The Salvos didn't want the law firms to lose their way and become normal-looking and normal-acting law firms. The Salvos also wanted to ensure that the people being hired had the same values as the Salvos—and only practiced the kind of law that the Salvos wanted them to practice."

But why two law firms?

"One funds the other," he replied. Salvos Legal Limited is a traditional commercial law firm run for the purpose of making a profit; those profits are then used to fund the operations of Salvos Legal Humanitarian Limited. The connection with the Salvos was also vital to getting operations off the ground. Besides providing initial seed funding of AUD$400,000, the Salvos also assisted Salvos Legal Humanitarian Limited with obtaining special charitable tax status: a status that provides employees of the firm with tax benefits. For example, after such tax benefits an annual salary of AUD$50,000 is worth the equivalent of about AUD$65,000-$70,000 at an entity without such status. Tax status was also one of the reasons behind creating two separate firms, as opposed to simply running one firm with a pro bono division. It also allows Salvos Legal Humanitarian Limited to accept donations and give receipts. Luke was quick to point out, however, that Salvos Legal Humanitarian Limited doesn't actively seek donations, although sometimes people do make them. Finally, on a more philosophical level, Luke believes that running the two entities separately enshrines a level of esprit de corps that wouldn't be found through separate divisions within a single entity. "Creating two separate entities with two separate brands reinforces that."

More important than seed funding or any charitable status was that the Salvos gave all its legal work to Salvos Legal Limited; this created immediate cash flow, and "got some early points up on the board. How would it look if we sought new work from a potential client and she asked if we did work for the Salvos—and we said 'no'?" As a result, Salvos Legal Limited began life with a good-sized client which it could showcase in search of more work.

In an era where many companies have corporate social responsibility targets and are looking for the fabled triple bottom line—(1) traditional corporate profits; (2) a "people account" showing how socially responsible the company is; and (3) a "planet account" showing how environmentally responsible the company is—this must have been an easy sell.

"Not so," Luke replied. "It was tough in the early days as we had to prove that we could do good legal work. Especially since Salvos Legal Limited was targeting the same big commercial clients and governments that every other law firm in Australia was targeting! Our strategy was to target clients that would give us a consistent flow of work, so we needed to show that we could handle volume work efficiently, and with a high degree of quality."

Salvos Legal Limited now counts Commonwealth Bank, as well as other banks, large Australian companies, and government entities, as its clients. "We also do 'moms and dads' work," Luke added. "We'll do wills, estates, and residential real estate matters."

It would not be hyperbole to state that the growth of Salvos Legal Limited has been explosive: 1000 percent growth in revenue over its first six years, with very little lawyer attrition. And in answer to those who believe that successful commercial law firms are no place for women, 80 percent of the firm's employees are women, and 50 percent of the firm's leadership are women. And as befits a commercial law firm, the administrative hub of the firm is based in Sydney.

However, sister firm Salvos Legal Humanitarian Limited is a very different matter. Its mission is to provide access to justice by representing those who could not otherwise obtain legal assistance—all at no charge. "We act in areas such as crime, family and children law, debt, housing, social security law, migration, and refugee law," Luke said. "And we select cases where we can make a difference in a person's life. It doesn't mean that we have to win every case; maybe we help them lose a bit better, or lose with dignity, help them to not be on their own, help them settle, help them win, or help to connect them with other services such as drug and alcohol services that will help show a court that they will not re-offend." Salvos Legal Humanitarian Limited is also clear about clients for whom it won't act. "We don't act for malicious people. People who have no desire to help themselves, or in family law cases where people are just trying to hurt each other."

This begs the question of client selection. "There must be an endless number of people who request free legal services," I said. "How on earth to you determine your clientele?"

Luke paused. His response was deliberate. "We try our best to assist all clients that come to us in a meaningful way, but we use a means assessment to determine what cases to take on. First we determine if the client can afford to pay for legal representation, or if there is another, more suitable, service available to which we can refer her. Then we ask, 'can we make a difference in this person's life?' In other words, 'does this client have a genuine desire to deal with the other factors that have brought them into conflict with the law?' Can we achieve a positive result in terms of rehabilitation, conflict resolution, advice and understanding, or in obtaining closure? And finally, is it consistent with the mission of the Salvation Army to act in this matter?"

Notwithstanding what seems like a complex protocol for determining representation, Salvos Legal Humanitarian Limited has acted for an astounding number of clients. Luke was understandably proud when he told me, "From our early days as Courtyard Legal to the end of June 2017, we've handled just under 19,000 humanitarian cases without the need for ongoing Salvation Army or government funding."

Very impressive, I thought. But I wasn't alone. In 2014, the prestigious *Lawyers Weekly* Australian Law Awards selected Salvos Legal as Australian Law Firm of the Year, "beating out every other law firm in the country, including national firms with global partnerships." And since then the awards have continued: Australian Boutique Firm of the Year, Australasian Law Awards 2015, Australian Law Firm of the Year (up to 100 lawyers), Australasian Law Awards 2016, and Innovative Firms, Australasian Lawyer 2016, among others.

It was hard for Luke not to smile as he told me. "But we're not stopping there. Our goal is to grow so that we reach 70 offices throughout all states and territories of Australia. These offices will employ around 140 lawyers plus administrative staff, and be supported by 700 volunteers."

I then asked the obvious question about how to manage a growing behemoth.

"We run both law firms as one social enterprise," he replied. Three senior managers from each side (Salvos Legal Limited and Salvos Legal Humanitarian Limited) meet regularly to make operational decisions relevant to both firms. Interestingly, these senior managers are referred to as "partners" despite the fact that they have no partnership interest. It seems that even in the most innovative structures, glorified titles from traditional law firm structures remain firmly in place.

The two firms share common policies, internal practices, and information (with appropriate privilege barriers maintained where necessary). The commercial firm is Law 9000-certified, a legal-specific version of the ISO 9001 standard, an arrangement that assists in properly and ethically managing confidential and privileged information. "Running the two firms as one social enterprise also gives everyone a sense of joint contribution. In this way, the commercial lawyers don't forget why they're there, and the humanitarian lawyers don't forget how it is they're able to be there."

Nonetheless, volunteers remain an important feature of both firms. As of July 1, 2017, the combined entity (Salvos Legal Limited and Salvos Legal Humanitarian Limited) operates from 16 locations between Sydney, Brisbane and Melbourne, plus provides a free national telephone service for people in rural and remote areas. The combined services are staffed by over 40 employees, and more than 250 volunteers, 60 percent of whom are lawyers. Volunteers are divided into two cohorts: a full-time cohort committed to a four-month stint at either Salvos Legal Limited or Salvos Legal Humanitarian Limited, and a part-time cohort solely for Salvos Legal Humanitarian Limited who volunteer at a drop-in centre or at an out-reach centre, "once a week, or once a month, or whatever it might be." It might seem odd that the Salvos would be able to find lawyers willing and able to volunteer for four months at a time, but Australia is currently flooded with junior lawyers and law school graduates who are unable to find work.

Like their full-time counterparts, volunteers only assist with the legal work for their selected entity. In other words, humanitarian volunteer lawyers only help with humanitarian legal work, and commercial volunteer lawyers only help with commercial legal work. The combined entities also take on a limited number of trainees from local law schools. Volunteers receive mentoring and access to all internal professional programs to help them develop their careers. Due to the combined entities' excellent reputation for training and legal experience, volunteers and interns receive a big leg-up when they seek full-time employment.

The head office on Castlereagh Street in Sydney is the only office where both firms work from the same place, the interior space of which, like its exterior, is utilitarian in design. Members of both firms work in an open-concept office space awash in neutral wall colours with the odd splash of colour coming from pictures or drawings in the desk areas.

The most remarkable aspect of the Sydney office décor is found in its small reception area. Sitting under a protective glass cover is a first edition of Salvation Army founder William Booth's 1890 best-selling classic, *In Darkest England and the Way Out,* which was gifted to Luke and his team by a generous donor. The large hardcover book is left open at pages 218 and 219—the beginning of section entitled "The Poor Man's Lawyer." Here one can read William Booth's vision for what Salvos Humanitarian has now become:

> *... men and women, weary and worn in the battles of life, need someone to whom they can go when pressed down with a sense of wrongs suffered or done, knowing that their confidence will be preserved inviolate, and that their statements will be received with sympathy ...*

> *I shall establish a department, over which I shall place*
> *the wisest, the pitifullest, and the most sagacious men and*
> *women whom I can find on my staff, to whom all those in*
> *trouble and perplexity shall be invited to address themselves.*

Only the hardest of hearts would not be inspired by these words as you encounter them day in and day out. If, as a lawyer, you were looking for purpose, there it was, in black and white. If, as a commercial law client, you were looking to give your fees to an entity with corporate responsibility and mission, there it was, staring you in the face as you waited in reception.

Given the success that this structure creates for paying and non-paying clients, as well as for society in general, I wondered how many other Australian charities had followed suit.

Luke gave me a sad smile.

"No one else in Australia is doing this. And even the Salvation Army in other countries has not tried to adopt a similar model. You really need the right people and the right champion to get this off the ground. We're highly supported by the senior leadership at the Salvos. And because of what I had done at Courtyard Legal, it was easy for them to see the outcomes and understand the stories of the lives that had been affected by our work."

"But it seems like the proof is in the pudding," I said. "Surely others in Australia will follow your lead."

"If another charity sets up a similar structure that would be fine by us," Luke said. "Every new player adds to access to justice and reduces the overall problem. We've done almost 19,000 cases, so if a few more charities came in and together we got that number up to over 100,000 cases, that's a good thing."

Impressions

It would be unfair to compare the Salvos legal enterprises to the process and technology-driven machine that is Slater and Gordon. What fascinated me about the Salvos enterprises was the funding mechanism—one that's not subject to the whims of donors or government largesse. In most countries, the knee-jerk reaction to the access-to-justice crisis is a cry for more or better government funding: a simplistic and unthoughtful approach that is doomed to fail when there are far more pressing government priorities.

The Salvos experience has clearly shown that legislative reform together with creative structuring is able to address access to justice in a way that's not a drain on public coffers; and that corporate social responsibility mandates can be the fulcrum which supports a self-funded model. As long as the Salvos can provide the same level of service as its competitors (and there is no reason why it can't), it will remain a differentiated proposition in the legal marketplace, one that no other commercial firm will be capable of emulating.

The key to replicating the Salvos entities (even in a tortured form for jurisdictions without enlightened regulators) is a consistent flow of legal work to the commercial firm. Without a constant flow of work, the entire operation is put in jeopardy. As such, the commercial firm needs to focus on those practice areas that have high, predictable volumes of legal work. One has to wonder therefore, when civic-minded corporations with a need for high volumes of legal service will seek out and work together with a charitable entity to replicate the success of the Salvos. Such a move could be the next evolution of corporate responsibility: moving from donations of time and money to the creation of an overall business strategy that simultaneously results in societal benefit.

Perhaps what's more likely to occur is that millennials will create variations of the Salvos model in other jurisdictions: creating mission-driven legal service providers filled with like-minded people who are driven by more than profit. Over the past decade, mission-driven companies have become a growing global movement, seeking to harness the energy and passion of employees to not only improve the bottom line but also to provide social benefit. Legal services has traditionally harnessed purpose-driven people of generation X, generation Y, and the baby boomer generation by creating legal aid clinics or non-profit organizations that eschew profit. Luke Geary saw another path: a truly "mission-driven" approach to commercial legal services where profits and purpose sit comfortably side by each. As a result, the Salvos entities represent the most significant generational shift in thinking about what a career in legal services is—and can be.

CHAPTER 3
RIVERVIEW LAW

"The Biggest Opportunity I've Ever Seen"

I first met Karl Chapman via Twitter.

Shortly after *Avoiding Extinction* was published, I received a private Twitter message from Karl, praising my book and asking for a phone call. A few months later I was taking a taxi from Liverpool to the Wirral offices of Riverview Law with a driver whose Scouse accent was so heavy the only thing I could decipher was "Guv'nor" at the end of many of his sentences. I hope he chalked up my perplexed looks and constant requests for him to repeat himself to my jet lag. Or maybe he just enjoyed my confusion. In any event, he eventually pulled into a small business park set back from the banks of the Mersey River and across the river from the John Lennon Airport. There was nothing flashy about the building. It was modern and purpose-built for business operations that don't need a prestige address. Riverview Law was not even a year old at that time, but it was already creating a real buzz in the UK legal marketplace.

Now, years later, I was again riding a taxi from Liverpool to the Wirral, more attuned to a Scouse accent and excited to visit a more mature and even more successful Riverview Law. Interestingly, Riverview Law traces its roots, not from legal services, but from a technology- and process-driven outsourced human resources company called AdviserPlus Business Solutions.

So, to understand the story of Riverview Law, one needs to first understand the story of Karl Chapman and AdviserPlus.

Karl is a serial entrepreneur. He began his career in the early 1980s as a fund manager for Guinness Mahon Investment Management before leaving to set up CRT Group PLC, a consultancy, recruitment, and training business. Under Karl's leadership his team grew CRT, both organically and by acquisition, to a market capitalisation of over £600 million, sales in excess of £400 million, and to a size of 2,500 employees operating from over 200 locations.

But Karl was always on the lookout for a new challenge. He could see throughout the 1990s that corporate human resources teams were under-resourced, ill-trained, prone to mistakes, and many seemed to be highly inefficient. Karl and his business partners saw an opportunity to use a proprietary combination of people, process, and technology to deliver outsourced human resources advice that was better, faster, and cheaper than creating a large internal human resources department. In 2001, Karl left CRT to set up AdviserPlus Business Solutions with a strategy of creating automated workflows to guide human resource decisions. It was a hit. Clients not only saw immediate cost savings, they also began making better human resource decisions. Karl's story may have ended there, but the law of unintended consequences had other plans.

From time to time, clients would say to him, "I really like this service. When are you going to move into legal?" And for many years, Karl brushed off the suggestion; he had studied law in university but he wasn't a lawyer. Moreover, legal services was a closed shop, open only to lawyers—and it all seemed rather complex. Besides, Karl thought, he had his hands full growing AdviserPlus.

But as the question was asked with increasing frequency, Karl reconsidered, especially with the passage of the United Kingdom's *Legal Services Act 2007*, which would permit non-lawyer ownership of law firms by the end of 2011. With new legislation removing a previously insurmountable barrier-to-entry, Karl saw huge green fields in legal services. It was a once-in-a-lifetime opportunity to use all the experience garnered from operating AdviserPlus and applying that knowledge to legal services. He knew that this would put a new offering miles ahead of the competition—and he decided to go for it. In early 2012, a new legal service offering, called Riverview Law, funded by Chapman and other AdviserPlus shareholders,[14] as well as a few partners of the global law firm DLA Piper, made its debut. The AdviserPlus experience clearly shaped Riverview's strategy and approach to the business of law. Riverview has "the DNA of a professional outsourcer, not that of a law firm," Karl explained. "We're capital-driven, not income-driven. So we're interested in long-term sustainability to get that capital back. This drives very different behaviour in terms of how we reward our people and how we invest in technology. It also helps us create a team ethic, rather than an individual ethic." A long-term, capital-driven approach to business is a fairly radical idea among law firms. Traditionally law firms seek to maximize income in each year (and then distribute nearly all of it), which incents short-term behaviour at the expense of long-term benefits.

---

[14] The initial incarnation of Riverview Law was a hybrid model of an outsourcing firm and a law firm, both of which were separate, but which were held together through a strategic alliance. In 2014, Riverview Law was granted an alternative business structures licence to fully operate as a legal services provider and the two separate bodies merged into one.

A Very Short History of Alternative Business Structures in the United Kingdom[15]

In March, 2001 the UK Office for Fair Trading published a study called "Competition in the Professions" which indicated that several elements of the legal profession (and other professions) were anti-competitive in nature; in particular it was concerned about rules barring outside investment in law firms.

Many UK lawyers opposed any change in regulation, claiming the profession was already very competitive amongst itself and so there was little need to introduce more competitors. They also feared that new structures involving "non-lawyers" would cause unethical behaviour and conflicts of interest, harmful to clients. Nonetheless, in 2002, the Lord Chancellor's Department, prepared a report titled, "In the Public Interest?' which indicated that the government was "keen to remove restrictive practices that are not in the public interest" and that "the professions should be fully subject to competition law."

Following this report, Sir David Clementi was invited to conduct an independent review. He published his final report, "The Review of the Regulatory Framework for Legal Services in England and Wales" in December 2004. The Clementi Report noted, among other things, that there was "considerable concern" over how client complaints were dealt with under the existing model, and that there was potential benefit to consumers if outside investment was permitted in English law firms. Allowing new business structures into the legal profession would encourage competition, innovation, flexibility and efficiency in service delivery, all of which would ultimately benefit consumers.

While the Clementi Report recommended a limited form of external ownership and investment (called, legal disciplinary practices, or LDPs), which would have capped "non-lawyer" ownership at 25%, the government of the day decided a more aggressive approach was needed and the Legal Services Act 2007 was born, creating alternative business structures (ABSs) with up to 100% "non-lawyer" ownership, subject to regulatory approval.

---

[15]   A more in-depth discussion of the history and debates in the UK over alternative business structures can be found in: Richard Devlin and Ora Morison, "Access to Justice and the Ethics and Politics of Alternative Business Structures," *The Canadian Bar Review* 91, no. 3 (2012): 483-553.

Unsurprisingly, given the close connection between the two companies, Riverview Law was opened in the building next door to AdviserPlus[16]—both within view of the Mersey River. Logistically, this allowed for shared IT and personnel while still maintaining appropriate confidentiality walls.

At its debut, the media and most of the legal market became "fixated" on Riverview Law's offering of fixed-fee pricing. But while fixed fees was then, and continues to be, a novelty in a legal services market obsessed with billing by the hour, fixed-fee pricing is nothing more than an outcome of Riverview Law's overall business strategy. In fact, Karl confided that he's quite happy for competitors to see Riverview's "secret sauce" as nothing more than fixed fees, or as some sort of temporary staffing business. "It gives us greater advantage when our competitors don't understand our model," he said. "Riverview Law is really a managed services outsourcing business, working hand-in-glove with clients as their partner over many years. Our pitch is simple. Outsource to us work that is of low or medium complexity, so that you can focus on the high-risk, mission-critical work. And we're absolutely confident that we can do that work better and at a lower cost."

Karl excitedly showed me around the office, pointing out how much had changed since I was first there in 2012: far more employees, an ice cream dispenser, and even new shrubbery dividing teams within the open office plan. And make no mistake, Karl Chapman is very excited about Riverview Law; he speaks quickly, and his energy and drive would put someone half his 55 years to shame—perhaps that's what keeps his physique lanky.

---

[16] In summer 2016, Karl Chapman and other shareholders in Riverview Law sold off their AdviserPlus shareholdings to focus all their attention on Riverview Law.

Walking around Riverview's offices, I could feel the youth and energy. Client teams were filled with young people eager to provide client services and fully empowered to question everything. No one was afraid to speak to Karl, or call him by his first name. In fact there was a great deal of ribbing during our tour and throughout the day. The success of this generation of employees at Riverview has caused Karl to make the bold statement that within five years, Riverview Law will stop hiring more experienced lawyers altogether—Riverview's growth will be entirely organic. "Culture is critical," Karl told me repeatedly throughout the day. And unlike traditional law firms, there isn't a culture of employee churn at Riverview Law. It's also why Riverview puts a great deal of effort into the selection and on-boarding of new employees—a process that is done monthly and takes a full week—to ensure that they are Riverview ready. "I want an employee to say, 'Wow, I've never been inducted like that before!'" Karl said. We settled into a boardroom where I continued to get the full Karl Chapman experience. As he spoke, his eyes twinkled behind thin-rimmed glasses. This guy loved his company and his job.

We discussed the state of the legal market as it applied to Riverview's target client: a corporation with large swaths of consistent, repeatable work. Historically corporations created a list or panel of outside law firms to whom work would be given. Sometimes these firms gave preferential fee pricing to the client in return for a place on the panel. But when the cost of outside law firms became too high, clients began building their in-house legal teams as a cost-saving measure. This amazed Karl. "What kind of a supply chain makes it cheaper for the customer to do the work itself? The legal supply chain is a mess! And on the client side, building an in-house team is nothing more than a short-term labour arbitrage play. We're the third option, an advisory outsourcer. We're a long-term partner, and as we do better, our costs reduce, and you give us more work." The premise seemed very logical to me. After all, in most industries, the better and more skilled the business is at a task, the faster and cheaper that task typically becomes.

So what does Riverview Law do that is so different in the delivery of legal services?

"We've not confused *management* with *ownership*," Karl said. "We're incorporated and our board—not individual lawyers—runs the company, taking into account the interests of shareholders and other stakeholders when making decisions. This structure also allows us to make decisions quickly so that we can move at pace." This sleek decision-making process was put to use fairly early in Riverview's life. The original company strategy was to focus on small- and medium-sized companies, with the hope that larger corporations would become attracted to the model over time. The uptake from clients, however, was the reverse: large corporations gravitated to Riverview faster than small- and medium-sized companies. As a result, Riverview soon abandoned the small- and medium-sized company market all together.

According to Karl, good technology and processes in combination with quality are the preconditions of success in any business, "but law firms never had to worry about that because of their protected status. Instead they focussed solely upon quality. Not technology, not process." I couldn't argue. Over time, that singular focus on quality makes for a whole lot of plain vanilla in the marketplace. There is no shortage of quality legal services in the UK, (or in most other first-world countries for that matter) which can make it hard for clients to differentiate among firms. As a result, law firms tend to be selected based on a "relationship" with a certain lawyer; likeability therefore becomes the differentiator.

This "relationship factor," however, reinforces to clients the value of the individual lawyer rather than the value of the team as a whole. It makes the client more portable, which is good for the lawyer, but not so good for the firm.

A team approach to legal services, coupled with technology, process, and use of data, creates strong business relationships between Riverview Law the *entity* and its clients—rather than personal relationships between a client and a specific lawyer at Riverview. Institutionalizing this relationship makes clients far more "sticky" and far less likely to move to another legal services provider. "In legal that sounds radical—but it's not radical in any other industry," Karl pointed out.

Dedicated teams of lawyers and staff build custom workflows specific to each client; no client is forced to use a static workflow that works for Riverview alone. As a result, the Riverview team actually blends with the client, making it "a true partner, not a supplier." To get the workflows right, the teams work backward from what a client wants or needs, as well as including what business insights Riverview thinks it can give the client, all of which determines what data needs to be captured. Lawyers are not the only employees who interact with the client. In fact, at Riverview it seems as if nearly everyone on a team has direct client interaction.

Karl was also clear that Riverview has no interest in being the largest law firm in the world. Its goal is to work with 20 to 30 global companies who can outsource a consistent flow of legal services to Riverview. Put simply, "We seek long-term contracts with blue-chip customers with high renewal rates." These long-term contracts allow Riverview to easily and accurately project cash flow, and to better plan investments. This different view of what a legal services provider should look like and act like has been successful for Riverview. "In the five years we've been running, we're already the same size as AdviserPlus after 15 years!"

Much like Slaters, there is a wide variety of career paths at Riverview Law. "We promote people through accounts, and some go across clients because of their activity and skill-set. Riverview Law has sales delivery teams dedicated to customers and within those we have client managers and legal managers, then teams, delivering the legal services," he said. Echoing Slaters' Andrew Grech, Karl told me that his job, and that of the other executives, is to make sure that all employees succeed. "Because then the company succeeds."

Each team has its own profit and loss account, and lawyers are measured by the quality of advice, timeliness of advice, and other things that make a difference to a client. There are six salary bands, each with a set of behaviours; Riverview does not use any form of lockstep advancement as it believes that "contribution and behaviours are more important than seniority."

Having a dedicated client service team allows Riverview to gather data and learn a great deal about its clients. He said, "We focus on the story that the data is telling us, such as the way customer operations are running so that we can save future costs and remove legal risk. We track data that will change the way client operations work, reduce costs, and make that function more efficient."

All of this data is translated into "management information" that is reported monthly to each client. "At first, clients understand that they need the MI," Karl said, "but are not quite sure how it can work for them. After we've been working with them for a time, the lightbulb goes on. As one of our clients told me, 'When I engaged Riverview I didn't realize that I bought the tip of the iceberg. I thought I was buying lower price, fixed-cost, dedicated teams and 24/7 access. But what you also did was help me understand how to free up my internal function, with management information, data, and your monthly reviews.'" It's no surprise then, that Riverview's reports continually improve, based on what it learns at the monthly client reviews.

"Data has become a big differentiator for Riverview Law and a huge value-add," Karl said. "We want to add value to clients through the information we're collecting since we're doing the legal work anyway. What information could come out of the work you're asking us to do that allows us to give you new insights into your business? And what information allows you to improve what your business does, to reduce its risk, to reduce cost, and improve performance?"

"The data tells a story," is what many Riverview employees told me throughout the day. "We use data to change behaviours." "Clients don't know what they don't know." "The more clients see, the more they want!" In fact there were a growing number of instances where Riverview Law was asked to sort and review clients' internal data, while other clients asked to use Riverview's technology internally. These requests led Riverview Law to create a consulting practice for clients that combines process improvement, workflow, and technology.

In building and tweaking products for clients, Riverview's IT team members work together with lawyers and other employees. Time and again, I heard comments such as, "we get ownership" and "it's exciting to be so involved with the process." One team member even used a very bad pun, welcoming me to "the centre of the legal Wirrald."

All of this means that Riverview is investing heavily in technology that is client-centric, not firm-centric. And that technology comes at a cost. In 2016, Riverview's research and development spend was about 20 percent of revenues, excluding internal salaries, clearly showing that Riverview has now morphed into what Karl called "a technology-led, patent-protected business that just happens to be in legal." From this vision has now sprouted a new strategy to productize Riverview Law.

"But wouldn't such productization cannibalize your existing business?" I asked, suddenly confused by what he had just told me.

"It's happening anyway," he replied with the matter-of-factness of someone stating the obvious. Karl believed that in the very near future, corporate customers would do even more of what's currently being done by the legal supply chain, because they'll have affordable access to the same tools "and they have a burning platform." Clients had been asking to licence Riverview's current technology for a few years already. So, in Karl's mind and the minds of the senior executive team, Riverview needs to be more than just a managed services or project services provider; in order to remain relevant, it had to become the partner of choice for corporate legal departments. And the best way to do that, the executive team believed, was through the creation of "a complete legal operations platform, a complete end-to-end manager for any legal work type." Named KIM, this platform combines artificial intelligence, workflow, process, management information and reporting, all on a "no-code" configurable platform; it sends complicated matters to the right legal person, and allows business teams to self-serve on less complicated matters.,

Far from cannibalizing business, it appears that KIM has actually reinforced the managed services and project services business lines. "It has not become an 'either-or' proposition," Karl said. "But rather an 'either-*and*' one." Clients who use KIM inevitably get more insight into their needs and operations, which then highlights areas where Riverview's managed services or project services can be of use. At this stage, the risk in productizing Riverview Law is paying off by reinforcing and strengthening the other business lines.

And like all of the legal innovators I interviewed, Karl was quick to note that Riverview hasn't got everything figured out yet, nor will they stop and rest on their success. "We're only at 50 percent of the journey," Karl said. "It's rare to get opportunities like this and this is the biggest opportunity that I've ever seen. I have the luxury of starting again with a blank piece of paper with all the lessons we've learned from our previous businesses, in a global multi-billion dollar market where customers are at a change point because they've had enough, the regulator has given us an opportunity to do something about it, and the existing competing infrastructure will find it very hard to compete against us. Now that we've been given this wonderful opportunity, we're having a great deal of fun with it!"

Impressions

Riverview Law, like other firms in this book, clearly benefits from the good fortune of being in a jurisdiction with forward-thinking regulators. More than just allowing outside capital, this jurisdictional benefit permitted the assembly of senior management who were unafraid to use their experiences from other industries to shape a new legal services provider. This previous experience also shaped the notion of how management views the business. There is no view that, "Gosh, law firms don't do that. We only do this." Its decision to create KIM is a prime example of how Riverview Law takes the widest possible view of what legal services is, and is unafraid to go wherever the market leads it. Management came to the conclusion that software may very well eat up wide swaths of legal work and decided to lead the market in this area, even at the risk of sacrificing other business lines. It was Riverview Law's corporate structure and focus on long-term decision-making (at the expense of short-term individual gain) that allowed it to react quickly and decisively. Few, if any, traditional law firms could quickly take that type of risk and make that kind of investment, without losing lawyers or practice groups; the focus on short-term gain at such firms would thwart any such attempt.

Much like Slaters, Riverview Law makes long-term investments in technology and process to build an entity-based approach legal services delivery, designing its service offerings to ensure client loyalty to the entity, rather than client loyalty to a particular lawyer or team member. Moreover, Riverview Law also understands that technology cannot be seen in terms of simply "keeping the lights on" and providing cyber-security; it's a very important part of creating a unique client experience. That's not to say that people are unimportant at Riverview Law. They're a critical element of the client experience and Riverview Law works hard to reduce employee churn, by investing heavily in the recruitment and induction process, providing diverse career paths, and by embracing a culture of continual improvement that gives team members a say in how they deliver services to clients—all of which are attractive to millennials. Existing law firms would do well to adopt Riverview's approach to technology, millennials, and long-term investment in order to create loyalty to the entity, rather than to individual lawyers.

Not to be lost in this discussion is the huge advantage that new players have over incumbent legal services providers: no legacy systems, no entrenched views, and no culture to change. Riverview Law started from a blank page and was free to create and execute on whatever strategy it saw as best in the marketplace, a strategy that I've seen change quickly and decisively over the past five years, an agility in decision-making that's remarkable and unheard of in traditional firms.

As I left Riverview, I started to extrapolate in my mind how, in a hyper-globalized and technology-driven world, geography becomes less and less important to legal service providers. And if that's true, then jurisdictions that do not amend their regulations to follow Australia, and England and Wales, place their own lawyers at a competitive disadvantage. After all, in theory, with the proper workflow, process, and technology an entity like Riverview Law could, provide legal services for global companies across a number of jurisdictions, all from the comfort of the Wirral. Perhaps I really *had* journeyed to the centre of the legal Wirrald.

CHAPTER 4

RADIANT LAW

"An incredible time with an incredible openness to new opportunities"

I'm often asked for career advice from law students at the University of Calgary. My answer is always the same: get hired by a law firm and milk that firm for all the experience you can get. Learn what works and, more importantly, what doesn't work. Then leave and create something better on your own. Radiant Law is a great example of what can happen if one follows that advice.

I had, like Karl Chapman, connected with Alex Hamilton over Twitter and, after some Skype conversations, I found myself in London exploring his upstart firm: a smaller version of Riverview Law that was also developing software and workflow to improve service. Alex has as good a legal pedigree as one can have: practicing as an IT lawyer at Norton Rose, Pillsbury, and then at Latham & Watkins, with on-the-ground experience in the UK, the United States, and South Africa—at both the associate and partner level. But no matter where he worked, Alex found himself surprised at how things got done in the large firm environment. Perhaps "surprised" is the wrong word; "amused" seemed to be a better characterization. But, unlike many lawyers who might have shrugged and kept collecting their draw cheques, Alex actually thought he could change things for the better. His first attempt to foster change in a big law firm came through technology.

After all, he was an IT lawyer with a fascination about the role of technology in legal services. He had some ideas that could improve firm operations and brought them to his law firm's IT department; the IT department ignored them.

Undaunted, he set up his own company to develop these ideas. "I then sold the new software back to my firm," he said with a big smile that then turned sour. "The IT department then rewrote it in twice the time—deleting half the features." The look of exasperation and disappointment on his face was one I had become familiar with when speaking to forward-thinking lawyers in many large-firm environments. "That experience gave me a very poor opinion of enterprise IT. For most law firms, IT is about getting a computer in someone's hands, and worrying a lot about security. Security is an all-consuming topic at law firms—that, and time-keeping systems—not innovation."

The financial crisis of 2008 put Alex's area of practice under heavy cost pressure, making it increasingly difficult to hit his fee-collection targets. In addition, Alex's hourly rate continued to climb every January. He knew that the market couldn't bear his ever-increasing rates for much longer. "My practice area was the next canary in the mine and if I couldn't innovate, I was in trouble. It was then that I sent out what I called my Jerry Maguire mission statement, setting out all the things the firm needed to do to remain competitive over the long run." Alex believed that law firm IT departments needed to move from a "keep the lights on" mentality to a builder mentality: that law firm IT departments needed to be heavily weighted with developers keen to make legal service products and to refine law firm processes.

"What was the reaction to that?" I asked.

"The firm thought I was insane, and nothing was done."

Yet Alex remained convinced there had to be a better way to deliver legal services and that technology would have a huge role to play. In January 2011, he left the life and salary of a global law firm partner to set up Radiant Law with four other co-founders (all of whom have since left), initially sharing office space with Greenberg Traurig Maher in Central London. Radiant Law eventually moved out to its own space closer to the Chancery Lane tube station. I met Alex at a small café not far from there to discuss Radiant Law and its role in the legal services marketplace. Unfortunately the day we arranged to meet was the morning after his birthday celebration—throughout our discussions I could see the pain behind his eyes.

Originally, Radiant Law had a two-pronged business strategy. "A boutique of outsourcing lawyers at fixed price in the truest sense: no time-sheets or time assumptions on our work," Alex said. He took a sip from his coffee and gently rubbed his temple. "That constraint on costs forced us to be smarter in how we worked on every file. Our other business line was high-volume commercial contracts or managed legal services."

Tasks within each file were assessed for risk and volume. Those bits that were low risk and high volume were outsourced. "We started with Pangea3 in India to do the junior work," Alex said, referring to the outsourcing provider. "Later we moved it to South Africa's Exigent." But the managed services line really took off and became a major growth engine for the firm. "In 2014, we decided to build our own outsourcing team in South Africa in order to bring that work back inside."

The firm's revenue continued to grow and the model seemed to have success written all over it. But Alex was quick to confess that in those early days, the founders were hugely naïve about what it took to run a growing multi-city organization. "One night in 2013, I literally woke up in a cold sweat. I had a nagging feeling that things were fundamentally wrong about our structure and operations." Radiant Law then hired business consultant Ciaran Fenton to take a look at their structure and help work through any necessary reorganization of the firm. Fenton's response to what he saw was unsettling—but instructive. "The only feckin' thing you've done right," Alex said, mimicking Fenton's Irish brogue, "is set up as a company." Fenton soon introduced Alex to Greg Tufnell, former CEO of publically-listed Mothercare who would become, and still remains, Radiant's non-executive Chairman (Tuffnell would also eventually become a minority shareholder). With Tufnell's guidance, Radiant Law converted to an alternative business structure "which gives us greater flexibility, greater access to management expertise and greater access to capital injections," Alex said. "Capital was vital to our initial growth plans. We wanted to put a dent in the market—and to do that you need scale. And to achieve scale, you need capital." As a result, Radiant Law operates under a classic corporate structure with formal managerial roles, commitments, and responsibilities. This included a re-alignment of current roles with Alex taking the reins as the full-time CEO and the creation of a proper, skills-based, independent board of directors. The new structure requires everyone at Radiant Law to be on salary, with an opportunity to earn a bonus based on metrics that are aligned with the firm's strategic plan.

"But we still have a long way to go," Alex admits. "We're building a plane in flight. We're constantly tweaking and getting better."

Much like Riverview Law, Radiant has again shifted its strategy. It no longer does boutique IT legal work and like Riverview Law, concentrates solely on managed legal services and project legal services (managing high volumes of contracts which are too complex for legal process outsourcers to handle). As Alex told me, "We're very focussed on how to improve contracting. There's not enough focus on objectives and business purpose, so we're about better meeting clients' needs as they create and manage their commercial relationships." He paused, gave his temple another rub, then continued. "In other words, why are we making things so hard in these commercial contracts? Can't we crystallize all this stuff, automate things that can be automated and focus on the real judgment-call components?" To this end, Radiant Law automates as much busy work as possible.

Radiant Law also seems to understand the needs of millennials. "I like young people who are enthusiastic," Alex told me sounding very much like Riverview Law's Karl Chapman. "As we build out our body of knowledge, our training programme, our competency model, and our staff induction programmes, we're increasingly able to take people and accelerate them up the learning curve. I often talk about dumbing down the work and raising up the people," Alex continued. "We invest in our people for the long term and the people we bring on board are those who have a higher comfort level with uncertainty than the average lawyer, but it's positive uncertainty. We want people who think about how to do things smarter all the time. As I tell all our new recruits, 'Amazing things are happening and you're going to be very much a part of figuring it all out.'"

I found it intriguing that Radiant Law has banned the use of internal email and uses team communication tool Slack as a way to communicate among themselves regarding projects and firm matters, which Alex told me increases employee engagement and improves communication. Employees also receive shares in the firm. Finally, Alex is true to his word about the team being part of figuring it out. He explained that he's slowly moving to a new organizational paradigm based on Frederic Laloux's book, *Reinventing Organizations*. A move that's already reaping benefits. In late 2016, Alex charged his team of about 30 (lawyers, developers, project managers and the like—82 percent of which are women) to sort out the best way to allocate work among themselves. Their solution? Pool all the work and let people self-regulate. As matters come in, "the team just jumps on them and now we've built a workflow system around that. The team loves it and jealously guards it. I'm in serious trouble if I ever try to change it!" That type of empowerment and trust is rare in traditional law firms and I could see why Radiant Law team members would guard it zealously. Now clients and law firms are asking to licence the same system.

Alex made it clear that the organization is always learning, and he sprinkled our discussion with a number of sound bites: "How do we get smarter?" "How do we add more value for the client?" "How do we re-engineer what we're doing?" "Every day we get a little bit smarter in figuring stuff out." I could see the attraction of working in a firm that's continuing to evolve and empowering its teams to drive that evolution.

As a result of its desire to automate busy work, Radiant Law has a number of software developers whose job is "to automate the hell out of everything!" The firm originally started by building its own software, then decided a better approach was to use and adapt generic software-as-a-service products from outside the legal industry, as well as working with specific legal technology. But even that approach only took Radiant Law so far. "Then there are a bunch of holes that drive you crazy and it's about how you can fill those holes," Alex laughs. "A lot of the software development involves making sure everything works together, so we've got pretty good at writing against APIs," referring to application-program interfaces, "and building things that plug into other things."

Like Karl Chapman, Alex sees technology, blended with the right talent, as the future of his firm and of legal services. The team is constantly building new workflows based on what worked or didn't work. "The way you do workflow really matters and we learn so much that we're continually improving and revising it." And, also like Riverview Law, Radiant Law is now licensing some of the software (such as RemarkableX) it created to fill the holes driving Alex and his team crazy.

"We live in an incredible time, with an incredible openness to new opportunities," he said when I suggested that Radiant is a good example of how smaller firms can now punch above their weight class. Although he originally felt that large capital injections were the only way to make a dent in the market, Alex now sees "an incredible collapse in the cost of setting something up." He said, "You can plug developers in and do interesting things at a fraction of the cost and twice the speed. But to really take advantage of it, you have to adapt practices and operate in an agile way, and continually re-invest in the business. To date, we've never taken money out of the business."

Impressions

Alex Hamilton saw the business opportunity of creating an entity that sits in a zone between full law firm services and very high level LPO-type services, but with the mentality of a software developer that doesn't waste the talents of employees on automatable tasks. And while Radiant Law's team approach to legal services is enviable, at its core is a strong understanding of what's important to its employees. Respect for employees by empowering them to take an active part in firm decisions, seeking constant improvement, and seeking to make work more interesting, while also improving client quality and reducing internal costs are critical to the firm's success – not lucrative compensation packages. Andrew Grech's words again echoed in my head, that success is "driven by people understanding purpose and feeling they have sufficient autonomy to influence that purpose and influence their ability to achieve that purpose." Alex was following those words even if he didn't realize it.

And like other firms in this book, Radiant Law is fortunate to be operating in a forward-thinking jurisdiction that allows it to take advantage of business expertise and capital from a diverse array of people, and that allows it to reward employees with shares in the business. The fact that Alex is the only remaining founder of Radiant Law (and previous departures have not destroyed the firm) is a testament not only to the strength of its structure, but also to the loyalty of clients to an entity, rather than to a particular person. Like Riverview Law, management agility is critical to allowing Radiant Law to move in and out of business lines at pace.

For law students, an important takeaway from the Radiant Law story is how a relatively small-sized operation (by number of people), started by a small group of lawyers with a big idea, can be successful in the Great Legal Reformation. Too often, there is a feeling that legal services is only for large players: that all the good ideas need massive scale and massive amounts of money. Radiant Law's story should also embolden legal entrepreneurs who may otherwise believe that these are the only paths to success.

CHAPTER 5
INVICTA LAW
"Unconquered"

The train ride from London to the county town of Maidstone seemed longer than it really was, running some fifty kilometres through the rolling fields and meadows of what is known as the Garden of England: Kent County. I had made the mistake of not bringing a book to read—staring at the neat fields only brought back unpleasant memories of going to law school in the farming heartland of my home province of Ontario.

A pleasant and fertile part of the country, Kent County has been inhabited for over 10,000 years, most recently by those with a defiant nature. In 1067, when William the Conqueror sought passage through Kent after the Battle of Hastings, the men of Kent rose up and blocked his way, threatening battle. Unwilling to engage in more bloody combat, William cut a deal that not only resulted in peace, but also created a proud motto for the Kentish: Invicta—unconquered.

Maidstone is an ideal location for a county town, situated along the banks of the Medway River on the old Roman road between Hastings and Rochester. The town has also had its share of historic excitement, whether during the Peasants Revolt of 1525, or 1648's Battle of Maidstone, or the burning at the stake of Thomas Hitton in 1530, the first English Protestant martyr of the Reformation.

But I was to see little of the town itself. Tiny Maidstone East train station is only a short walk up the hill to the Edwardian grandeur of the Kent County Council offices. Three Union Jacks waving in the slight breeze, cobblestones, and a massive arch all led me to an inner courtyard. I was so impressed by the architecture—one that befits the offices of one of the largest counties in England—that I spent more than 20 minutes wandering about the place soaking up history and pretending to look like I knew exactly where I was going. Eventually I asked for proper directions and was guided to Kent County Legal Services.

A visit to an in-house municipal legal team may seem an odd choice for a book about legal innovation. After all, it's easy to dismiss government legal teams as the place where lawyers go when they want a less-stressed, cozy lifestyle. I remember several of my former colleagues in municipal legal departments tirelessly working out their retirement formula, factoring in all contingencies so as to know the precise day on which they could move out with maximum pension. After all, what's the incentive to work harder when you have a captive client, a comfortable benefits plan, and little annual bonus potential?

I had been introduced to Geoff Wild and his vision for the Kent County legal team while I was in London several years before. I was intrigued by his desire to prevent the caricature of public sector lawyers from conquering the souls of his team and I had been following the transformation of his team ever since. Now was my chance to "look under the hood."

"It was 1997 and I was fresh into the job as Head of Legal," Geoff said, taking a seat on the other side of a small table in his massive, high-ceilinged office. His smooth, velvet-like voice worked well with his height and square jaw; he had motion-picture leading man written all over him. "Just 36 years old, and promoted over my boss into the role. I had never had a managerial role, but I had worked in a number of other organizations and seen how the good ones were run—and how bad ones were run."

The group Geoff was asked to lead was a small team of 25 lawyers. The words "disjointed" and "chaotic" flowed as Geoff described what he had inherited. The team hadn't any sense of direction, management, or "purpose in life other than to churn work through the sausage machine. As a result it was hugely inefficient and clients were dissatisfied—yet they were forced to use these lawyers without choice." He paused. "And the lawyers knew that, so they could give whatever level of service they wanted."

The in-house team had been kept small at that time, and great swaths of legal work were sent to outside law firms at great cost to the county. There was no performance management, productivity, customer satisfaction, or quality assurance—none of the basic building blocks of a good legal practice were in place. "And there was no encouragement or incentive to do things any differently," Geoff said. "The clients were so unhappy that they wanted everything sent to outside law firms."

"That's a pretty grim picture," I said. Although it was not entirely surprising to me.

"Don't get me wrong, Mitch. I'm passionate about the public sector and I feel that it's very important—I just didn't like the way that it worked. It's hugely inefficient, hugely wasteful and lacking in all sorts of things that one finds in abundance in the private sector. So I thought, why can't we borrow all the best bits from the private sector and, with a great big hypodermic needle, inject them into the public service and create the best of both worlds?"

He paused to take a sip from his glass of water. "Then you would have the private sector mentality— their ways of working, models of customer relationship and client development, and business practice—all within a public sector environment where your entire focus is on improving the lives of the people you serve, in the communities where you live."

"How on earth do you turn that type of situation around?" I asked. Sadly, the answer is that one needs a good bit of luck.

"In government," Geoff said, "if you catch the right wind you can really go places." And in Geoff's case, it seems that he caught a wind of hurricane force—but in a good way. The county had just elected a new council, and a new leader. In addition, the new chief executive, to whom Geoff reported, was someone of vision and openness. To further invigorate the spirit of change management, neither of these leaders had been brought up in the public sector, freeing them from any legacy trains of thought. It was truly a once-in-a-lifetime chance. In Geoff's mind, this was now an environment where anything was possible. Fully backed by leadership, Geoff was encouraged to ask hard questions, put forward fresh new ideas, and challenge the status quo.

But there was clear time pressure. The county's chief executive gave Geoff an ultimatum, much like what one sees in an action movie where the hero is given one last chance to prove he's right. "You've got one year to redesign and remodel the in-house legal team or, you can oversee its complete externalization." Basically, shape up or ship out.

So off he went.

Geoff was convinced he could win back the outsourced work by doing it just as well, if not better than, the outside law firms— but at a fraction of the price. He laid out his vision to the team and began ruthlessly working toward his goal and to his timetable. "There was no room for passengers on this journey" Geoff said, and so, over the first 18 months,[17] he lost 75 percent of his original team. Most had left and "some had to be helped onward. They weren't up for the journey and I needed every person in every position to be pulling in the same direction."

At the same time Geoff was "massively recruiting," personally sitting in on every interview to ensure that all new hires were the right "fit." The concept of "fit" is often bandied around by traditional law firms, but rarely taken very seriously. Geoff, however, had seen first-hand how disruptive hiring the wrong person could be. "One wrong person can have a tremendously damaging effect on the team. Having to deal with that negative situation later on is far more difficult than the time involved in sitting in on interviews in the first place." His approach reminded me of the old carpenter's adage: *measure twice, cut once.*

Perhaps most astounding in the law firm hiring process is that Geoff doesn't ask prospects any questions about law. "I assume a certain level of legal ability, but if it isn't there, I can teach it. I've learned the hard way that choosing legal skills over soft skills is a mistake." In fact it's not unusual for Kent to go through a search process and, after interviewing all candidates, decide that not one is a fit—meaning the process will need to continue.

This painstaking search process forces Geoff to be deeply embedded in understanding the demand for legal services so he can accurately forecast where the need for more lawyers will come from, and to have the search process planned well in advance, so that few gaps needed to be plugged with locums.

---

[17]   Geoff Wild was able to show some early results and savings within the original 12-month mandate, and was therefore able to buy more time to continue implementing the transformation of his team.

The tactics worked. Soon Geoff and his group were handling 95 percent of Kent County Council's legal work.

"Give me more details," I pressed. "There's got to be more to it than simply cutting out the deadwood and hiring true believers. Surely there needed to be some structural change as well." I worried that this was all there was to it. In which case, as pleasant as Maidstone was, my trip here had been a bust.

"The biggest structural adjustment," Geoff told me, "was a change in the funding arrangement." Government departments around the world are given a budget each year for the legal team. The budget for Kent County Legal was no different. Every year it was given a budget for the salaries of its lawyers and other team members, as well as for other sundry costs. The budget, however, was not based on demand, usage, need, or capacity. It was based on historic budgets "that bore no resemblance to reality."

Having a guaranteed pot of money from which to draw from may have been comforting for those within the legal team, but it also meant that the legal team didn't have to do very much to earn that money. The money arrived every year, come what may. It didn't grow, but it also didn't shrink to any great degree. There was no incentive to save money, and if lawyers were unable to get to certain files, these files were pushed out into the following year—with no desire to create and maintain client satisfaction.

Geoff's solution? He gave the budget back—at least notionally.

What would have been the legal department's budget was notionally given back to the county and divided among those departments that used legal services. Now Kent County's in-house lawyers started each year with no money—and no work. "I didn't want the clients to come to us if they didn't want to," Geoff said. "I took the shackles off the clients and let them go elsewhere if they were unhappy with our team."

With the safety net taken away, the lawyers now had to justify their role or the clients would go elsewhere. The legal department also had to work hard to reduce their costs to ensure that they could win work from their own internal clients.

"We became efficient and lean," Geoff said. "We focussed on costs, efficiency, and customer care because, quite frankly, our jobs depended on it!" Soon internal clients were able to receive good, cost-efficient service from the in-house team. They began to better appreciate the lawyers and involved them more in situations that mattered, rather than in things that didn't matter.

This change also created a different mindset with clients. Previously, clients considered the Kent County Legal team to be a "free service" which allowed clients to take the team for granted. In some cases, clients were sending nearly every agreement or decision to the legal department because they didn't understand the value of the work done by the legal team. "It was an unhealthy relationship between lawyer and client," Geoff recalled. He also re-jigged the team's hourly rates to reflect actual costs, so internal clients better understood the true costs of the team—and its true value. The result was that internal clients became more discerning and the legal team got better legal work. Some clients also determined that their budget for legal work was woefully inadequate.

But then something unexpected happened: Kent County's in-house legal team's income began to grow beyond its costs. As income grew, the in-house team could expand. Not long after, a number of legislative amendments to the Local Government Act 2003 and the Solicitors' Practice Rules allowed the Kent County legal team to undertake legal work for other counties and towns. Geoff had unintentionally created England's first captive municipal law firm, and possibly the only one of its kind in the world: all of it cost neutral to Kent County.

With the team now working for outside clients, the imperative to truly operate as a lean, efficient business became even greater. The team was now directly competing with private law firms in a market of over 450 local authorities that had an annual legal services spend of £1.0 billion. By the end of 2016, the team had become an important profit centre for Kent County, contributing an annual net profit of approximately £2.6 million by working for over 600 other government bodies across England. This was £2.6 million of additional revenue that could be used to fund other programs across Kent County. Internal legal teams, in both the private and public sectors, constantly struggle with how to demonstrate their worth to those holding their purse strings. How to be seen as something more than a necessary evil? In some eyes, Geoff had found the Holy Grail, providing the best and most convincing return on investment: profit.

While one rarely hears the word *innovative* when it comes to municipal government legal departments, one certainly never hears the word *profit*. "You'll leave a wonderful legacy," I told him.

"Mitch, we're not done yet. We can't stand still," he said. "Our traditional client base is shrinking due to government budget cuts. The legal profession is changing, and even the public sector is changing, so we must change before we're forced to change. We need to reinvent again, because anyone who believes that we can keep doing the same thing ten years from now is fooling themselves. If we don't adapt and reinvent again, we'll be overseeing our own decline."

Geoff then told me that the Solicitors Regulatory Authority of England & Wales has been slowly reducing the type of work that his in-house team could provide and this turn of events, combined with budgetary pressure on many of Kent's clients, threatened to shrink his group. Despite all the prior success, Geoff could no longer grow his business or his team.

Then he leaned in and told me about the next evolution of Kent County Legal Services. "We've recently converted to an alternative business structure that's wholly owned by Kent County. Later in 2017 we'll be moving from these historic walls and into a new, modern and completely open plan workspace— just a few blocks from here on Union Street. And teams will have full mobility to work from anywhere in the world."

"And the name of this new beast?" I asked.

"Invicta Law. In keeping with the Kentish tradition of victory!" he laughed.

The new entity will keep Geoff Wild as CEO and will sign a ten-year contract with Kent County to ensure long-term consistent cash flow. He believed that the new entity would bring massive value to clients, give the legal team a national footprint, and also provide better career advancement opportunities for his team, which had grown to 160, including 125 fee-earners. In its current form, Kent County Legal Services doesn't have enough places for people to advance—it had lost good people, and would continue to do so. "If you attract ambitious people who want to adapt and be creative, they need outlets," Geoff said. "That's part of what the iteration into an ABS is all about."

Geoff had convinced the County Council to spin out the legal department by showing how a new structure would be better, faster, and cheaper. High on his list was heavy investment in a technology platform that would not only reduce the number of touches the team would make to a file (thereby reducing errors and time spent), but also create a client portal that would improve client accessibility and service. Like the executives at Slaters, Geoff believed that technology would have a profound effect on his operations. So much so that he famously[18] stated to the county council that the new entity will not be "a legal business that happens to use technology. Instead, it will be a digital business that happens to do law."

The investment in technology, however, was not one that the county would be able to afford if the team stayed in its original form. Spinning the legal team into an ABS would allow it to tap into a greater range of funding. Being better, faster, and cheaper would not only create an even more profitable entity, it would create a county asset that would appreciate in value over time, giving Kent the option of selling all or part of Invicta Law for a healthy gain. The new entity would also allow Geoff to experiment with new opportunities, such as "white labelling" certain routine legal work for private law firms.

"I want to make an impact," he told me. "I think the market is ready for it. And I want to continue to be part of something that is breaking new ground, doing something different, and carrying on the journey that I've been on for these last 20 years. And because," he smiles widely, "it's just a lot of fun!"

Ben Watts (then head of the Litigation and Social Welfare Team) decided not move to the ABS but would stay on as general counsel to Kent County along with team of eight (including six lawyers) to form what Geoff calls the "Intelligent Client": a client that not only makes better use of its talent, but also purchases and manages legal services in a more modern and intelligent manner. Ben had spent years working as a buyer for a wholesaler to pay for

---

18   Neil Rose, "'A digital business that happens to do law'–is this the future?" *Legal Futures* (September 28, 2015): http://www.legalfutures.co.uk/latest-news/a-digital-business-that-happens-to-do-law-is-this-the-future.

law school, a job that was not only lucrative, but also gave him a good perspective on legal services. "The legal market thinks it's different, but it's not," he told me. "It's selling boxes. And you've got to make that box a compelling offer. Just saying 'buy me because I'm a red box' is not good enough."

Even before the conversion to an ABS, Geoff's team had been looking at the fusion of technology and human interaction very closely. "We've been investing in technology, workflows and automation," Ben said, "trying to sort out how we can get technology to do more. The difference between ourselves and a traditional law firm is that traditional firms see technology as purely a cost-saving measure: if I do this, the cost can go down. Whereas we look at technology and say, yes the cost can go down, but how can it improve the service we're providing to the client? We want a true partnership with our clients and that concept is integral to our processes and thinking."

"There's also an element of survival and business development about it," I suggested.

"True, but it comes from a different perspective. We want to make our clients better, and if making them better means that they need us less, then we've done our job. It's all part of our natural evolution."

"Was that what kept you at Kent County?" I asked.

"We kept reinventing ourselves and that kept me here. I could earn more money elsewhere, but it's the intellectual freedom to be myself that kept me at Kent," Ben said. "You're expected to *not* be a traditional solicitor here, and I like that!"

Throughout the day I heard time and again that all ideas are equally valid to Geoff; ideas are evaluated based on their merits rather than based on the person who brought it forward; and people are encouraged to bring new ideas and create new opportunities for themselves and for others. And, like other forward-thinking firms, Geoff and his senior team work hard to ensure people are empowered to provide their ideas and to try anything.

One lawyer I spoke to told me that his practice area was not one that actively sought out work from other government bodies; in fact, his group had so much work from Kent County that it generated the most internal fees each year. But he was quick to note that "Geoff's model gives us stability in the services we deliver. The model allows us to recruit and retain people according to our needs and to deliver the service that my clients demand. It's when you're sent into battle with one hand tied behind your back that morale plummets. In this model, we're masters of our own destiny."

Another told me, "We're always looking to evolve, change, and be more dynamic. That gives someone like me the chance to deliver a high quality service which is greatly appreciated and it also gives me a lot of professional satisfaction. It would take a lot to entice me away, but everyone has their price!" He laughed. "Autonomy is key here and Geoff is trailblazing, so why would I leave? I'm stimulated and stretched here."

"Stretched," "challenged," "exciting," "open," "empowering," "flexible" were all terms that came up in many of my discussions with Kent County's in-house team. Sometimes lawyers were caught off guard by the openness of the model. As one said, "I suggested to Geoff that we needed better technology in our group. He said, 'Okay, then you look into that and handle it.'"

Geoff's humility and openness were refreshing and genuine. "I'm a great believer in surrounding myself with better people than I myself. I'm a simple guy; I want to make my life as easy as possible. If my life is made easy because I have fantastic people around me, then the engine's purring at that stage. If all I want is to be surrounded by people who never challenge me—suddenly my life is a helluva lot harder. I don't want to be carrying this on my own. I want people to carry it themselves because then they're as fired up for it as I am, or more so! I love that there are people here who want to take this in a direction that I've never even thought of!"

Impressions

Completely redesigning the revenue model for the in-house team at Kent County was a huge risk for Geoff Wild to take; it was a decision made easier by the fact that he was forced to take it. Fortunately, this new revenue model gave him the freedom to rethink what services should be delivered, and how they should be delivered. In redesigning his team to emulate a more commercially-minded enterprise, Geoff was able to take advantage of regulatory reforms that increased revenues and attracted legal talent.

And while the legal team retains a more traditional hierarchy in form, culturally it appears that no such hierarchy exists; ideas are evaluated on merit rather than seniority, thereby allowing every generation within the firm to feel it is empowered and able to make valuable contributions to the entity. Geoff's commitment to creating interesting, varied, and long-term careers for employees dovetails with his desire to ensure the entity is well-positioned for long-term survival and to be the master of its own future. Not surprisingly, Geoff sees the importance of technology to not only assist his team deliver quality legal services in an accessible and cost-effective manner, but also to improve his team's quality of life.

Like other innovators in this book, Geoff understands that his team is on a journey that's closer to the beginning than to the end. As a leader, Geoff Wild is not a caretaker or a tinkerer. He has a vision and he feels a strong responsibility, not to personal aggrandizement, but to ensure that his teams have what they need to provide service to his community as well as to ensure that his teams have the best possible career opportunities. What deeply impressed me about Geoff was this two-pronged approach to building his legal service vision: it had to be good for the client, but it also had to be good for his team. The two were always to be intertwined.

There are few leaders of government legal teams who have the vision, courage, and conviction to take their teams back into the private sector, and into a new model. So the story of Kent County Legal Services and its metamorphosis into Invicta Law is as much a story of leadership as it is a story about innovation. The ongoing story of Invicta Law should be a critical blip to watch on every legal innovator's radar screen for the doming decades.

And while there may be public sector lawyers who dismiss Invicta Law as something unattainable outside of England, that would be a mistake. There's no shortage of public sector legal departments staffed with personnel having little incentive for change and whose morale is crushed by budgetary constraints. And while there may be regulatory barriers to prevent some departments from completely replicating Invicta Law's metamorphosis, imaginative leaders will take pieces from the Invicta story and mould them in ways that improve their departments.

PART TWO

PROCESS, PROCESS, PROCESS

CHAPTER 6

HUNOVAL LAW

"The Power of the Idea"

Imagine it's 2009 and you're a young female paralegal living near Charlotte, North Carolina. You're seeking a move from your current position because you feel "stuck." You want to grow professionally and learn new things, but your law firm's not providing you with any of that. You begin searching for new opportunities and new ideas—you want a place where you can be challenged and grow. In the meantime, New England media outlets are beginning to report on a series of brutal attacks and eventually a murder, perpetrated by an unknown assailant they've dubbed "the Craigslist killer."

Cara Clausen laughs with embarrassment as she continues the story. "I happened upon a Craigslist job posting for a paralegal with experience in foreclosure work at a small, new law firm. With a bit of hesitation, I arranged a meeting—in a very public place—with Matt Hunoval. My family knew exactly where I was, and how long I should be there. Soon after that, I became the first official hire of the Hunoval Law Firm."

Notwithstanding the grim news from up north, "Matt did all his job postings on Craigslist during our first year of operation," Cara recalls. "Like all start-ups, we ran on bubble-gum, tin foil, and duct tape for that first year or two!" She laughs at the absurdity of it all. "Lean Six Sigma was nowhere in the picture at that time. We were just trying to survive and gain a foothold in the business. There we were; me and Matt sitting back-to-back typing foreclosure documents in a tiny office—a one-client firm." Those humble beginnings would not last long. The firm's growth would soon explode and reach a high of about 100 full-time employees, including attorneys, doing work across North Carolina, South Carolina, and Virginia.

*   *   *

For some time, I had heard rumblings of this small southern law firm and its use of Lean Six Sigma to drive efficiency and quality, and to gain competitive advantage over its law-firm peers. As it happened, my wife and I were visiting her family in Atlanta, Georgia, an easy three-hour drive from Charlotte. After spending an acceptable number of days with family, I followed I-85 up to North Carolina to better understand what in the world Matt Hunoval was up to.

Charlotte itself is a wonder: bits of the Bible Belt, NASCAR, and southern charm all rolled up into a high-energy modern metropolis whose skyline is continually changing. As an avid baseball fan, my mouth watered as I drove by BB&T Park, set in the heart of downtown. I had hoped that the Charlotte Knights would have a home game while I was there—but they didn't.

I hadn't put much prior thought into where Hunoval Law's offices were exactly located. I assumed they would be somewhere around downtown Charlotte, nothing too swanky, but still hip and cool. Such is life in a world of GPS that after I finished salivating over BB&T Park, I simply input the office address and drove on. As I found myself driving *away* from downtown to the industrial outskirts of Charlotte, I realized that Hunoval Law was going to be a very different kind of place.

Hunoval Law's offices are intentionally low-key and unremarkable—situated in a small, well-treed business park not far from the southernmost end of the Billy Graham Parkway, close to a Blue Line transit station and a major industrial plant. The squat two-storey brown brick building is nestled among plumbing supply stores and other commercial businesses. This location definitely saves a great deal in rent, I rationalized, as I pulled into the parking lot. I would later find out that Matt had actually bought the entire building to accommodate the steep growth trajectory of his firm.

Like most small firms, Matt Hunoval financially "bootstrapped" the entire operation on his own, so it was critical to keep overhead as low as possible; I encountered no oriental rugs, fancy artwork, or majestic city views. Office space at Hunoval Law is not a shrine to anyone; it's strictly utilitarian. The management structure of the firm is also quite lean. Hunoval Law isn't a partnership, it's a corporation wholly owned by Matt Hunoval and his wife, lawyer Christi Hunoval. Matt is CEO.

First, some background on Hunoval Law: it's not a "full-service" law firm. It specializes in mortgage foreclosure work and in residential real estate transactions. "I made an early strategic decision *not* to be all things to all people," Matt told me, while he finished up some paperwork. Matt had a linebacker's build and was clad, like most of the firm, in a polo shirt and chinos. Matt brought his own personal touch to his office, filling it entirely with furniture having a shiny metal aviator-style finish. Somewhat unconventional in a southern American state where I imagined lawyers still revelled in dark mahogany finishes.

"To make informed decisions that lead to success in any endeavor," he continued, "you've got to first fundamentally understand who you are—what are your strengths, what are your weaknesses." His voice was clear, measured, and focussed. "As a small firm, we could have just been another average law firm going the general practice route. Instead, I decided to maniacally and singularly focus on a small area and be the very best at it: real estate."

Matt understood that a key component to being the "very best" would be the underlying machinery that, as Andrew Grech had told me on the other side of the planet, would allow his team to go for gold. In 2012, Matt connected with consultant Kevin Divine to set up Hunoval Law with a cloud-based technology infrastructure, enabling the firm to quickly scale up, or down, as needed. In theory, the firm could move to another location overnight. And its cloud infrastructure meant that the firm only paid for the services it needed without long-term commitments, allowing the firm to remain nimble and to react quickly.

As all good technology consultants know, process is the foundation of any technology project. "You can't create a technology solution until you understand what process you're trying to enable," Kevin told me later that day. Kevin, a Six Sigma Black Belt, had spent ten years at General Electric, before moving on to the banking sector in 2007, then to work with a local consulting firm in 2009. It was in trying to understand Hunoval Law's processes that Kevin started to make process improvement suggestions. Soon, this steady stream of suggestions evolved into a formal engagement to undertake full-blown process improvement at Hunoval Law.

"Technology was the foot in the door," Kevin recalled. "It wasn't business process improvement or Lean Six Sigma. But once we were able to show some dramatic improvements—we cut one process from 90 days to less than nine—Matt liked that. He's a visionary, and he immediately saw how process improvement could be a key market differentiator for him."

"I thought about what Kevin was saying about process improvement for a few weeks," Matt Hunoval said. "Lawyers tend to think they're the smartest people in the room and some of Lean Six Sigma—the coloured belts for different levels of proficiency—seemed gimmicky offshoots of karate." After talking with Kevin, Matt did his own independent research on Lean Six Sigma. He knew that Six Sigma was a set of tools and techniques created by Motorola in the mid-1980s to eliminate or reduce variations in its products: a system so successful that it was adopted across a wide variety of industries, including companies such as IBM, Boeing, Verizon, and General Electric. Lean, on the other hand, was pioneered by Toyota as a set of tools and techniques to simplify and speed up work processes by eliminating wasteful steps or actions. Lean Six Sigma combines both sets of tools and techniques to "do the right things [and only the right things] (Lean), and [to do] those things right (Six Sigma)."[19] While each system has its own jargon, techniques, tools, and certifications, the over-arching and unifying theme behind them is to create a culture of improvement. At the time, Matt hadn't seen any law firm in the American South make the leap to fully implement any of these ideas.

---

[19] Catherine Alman MacDonagh, "Deliver Value through Legal Lean Sigma and Project Management," in Legal Procurement Handbook, ed. Silvia Hodges Silverstein (Buying Legal Council, 2015): 24.

Matt also saw a clear connection between processes in large corporations and the processes at his firm. "The pejorative term for a high-volume, process-driven practice like ours is that we're a mill. Good, bad or ugly, there's a kernel of truth to that. And so the great 'Aha!' moment was when I realized that this discipline, which had been so enormously successful in the manufacturing context, could have significant conceptual overlap with what we do at our 'mill.'"

At this point of our discussion I began to see flashes of the evangelical Matt Hunoval, something that I would see throughout my time in Charlotte. "I'm a big believer in the power of 'The Idea' and when I ask my staff why we do things a certain way and the answer is 'that's how it has always been done' or 'that's how we did it at the firm I used to work for'—it makes my skin crawl. That's a non-answer to me."

He continued, "We ran some small-scale pilot projects which far exceeded my loftiest expectations—then there was no looking back. I wanted us to be the best we can be at what we are." When I talked to Hunoval Law employees about the concept of Lean Six Sigma, it was repeatedly stripped down to "forcing you to think of what you're doing as a matrix or a puzzle, then allowing you to rethink how the pieces fit together, and to question if all the pieces are really necessary." In short, this philosophy forces employees to think about what they do in a more critical manner, forcing them to take ownership of their work. There is also the obvious operational benefit. If an employee is able to remove a few minutes from working on a file, it may not seem like much, but if those few minutes are multiplied by the hundreds of files she works on, that can really add up!

The huge competitive advantage that Matt saw in making Lean Six Sigma the cornerstone of his firm's operational strategy was one thing. Implementing it was quite another. Not a single law firm in the Bible Belt, or, for that matter in any other part of the country, was doing what Hunoval wanted to do. (Little did he know that Seyfarth Shaw was attempting something similar about 500 miles north of Charlotte, but more on that later) There was no roadmap, no blueprint. Matt would be hacking a new path through the jungle with nothing but a machete. He had two options for finding a way through the jungle: rely upon outside consultants to train employees, or bring the required expertise in-house. Matt chose the latter, which proved to be critical to ensuring consistent implementation and monitoring of the new program.

"It's actually not very hard to complete a project and see immediate results," Kevin told me. "The hard part is sustaining results. To do that, you need to constantly monitor and track the system, and have someone continually driving change. If Matt had gone with an outsourced approach to managing Lean Six Sigma, it's very likely that the initial success would have deteriorated. The old processes and ways of doing things would have eventually returned by sheer institutional inertia."

But whom to train? Again Matt had two options; train the lawyers and top executives in the hope of a trickle-down effect to the staff, or train the staff and work upwards. Again he chose the latter. After all, people in the trenches have far better visibility into day-to-day processes than upper management. But training tens of people comes with a huge financial price tag. At the time, the average cost to send one person for Lean Six Sigma training through a nationally recognized credentialing programs was running at about USD$5,000 per person—far out of Matt's budget.

The vision of Hunoval Law as a Lean Six Sigma pioneer in the legal industry might have died there, if it had not been for the Center for Lean Logistics and Engineered Systems (CLLES) at the University of North Carolina at Charlotte. CLLES had a strong focus on Six Sigma training across multiple industries— just not for legal services. It didn't take long for Matt to convince CLLES of the potential benefit of working with a legal services sector that was worth about USD$500 billion a year in the United States alone: a service sector that had been untouched by process improvement. A partnership between CLLES and Hunoval Law was soon cemented to create a customized legal Lean Six Sigma course co-designed by Kevin Divine and CLLES: one that was specific to Hunoval Law, using the firm's own real-world, day-to-day processes and procedures as the curriculum. One of the benefits of partnering with CLLES and bringing the Lean Six Sigma process in-house, Kevin told me, "was that we could simplify it and tailor it to what we, as a law firm, actually do. There's no need to use every tool in the tool box. We just use the tools that are right for the job—and only those tools."

At the time of my visit, about 60 percent of all Hunoval Law employees have gone through the CLLES program and earned their Green Belts. "We'll probably never get 100 percent," Matt confided. "But we want to get as close as possible. It's a cultural transition as much as it's an operational one, and so, to optimize buy-in and efficiency, we need a critical mass of people who understand the language we're speaking and what we're about."

Each fiscal quarter, five Hunoval team members take the Green Belt Lean Six Sigma class at CLLES. The class runs all day, every Friday for five consecutive weeks. And while students are not required to make up any lost time from work, they *are* required to pass an examination at the end of the course. Once they're fully grounded in the Lean Six Sigma theories taught at CLLES, students return to the firm to come up with a process improvement project for their area of work. This typically involves mapping all the steps of a process in which they're involved, determining "pain points," or things they wish they could change to make the process run smoother or faster, then spending the next 60 days implementing a solution.

And, like all champions of change management, Hunoval Law celebrates those who support the firm's transformation by organizing formal graduation lunches where students are recognized in front of their peers. They each receive graduate certificates, as well as an actual green belt, embroidered with their class year and name. In fact, it has now become a Hunoval Law tradition for every graduate to hang her belt near her workspace.

It seemed to me that if process improvement plays a large role in a firm's success, then it would also change the dynamics of the firm. At traditional law firms, everyone in the firm defers to the lawyers in terms of how to complete files and how to service clients; and among lawyers, associates defer to partners. However, with a process-driven approach, I envisioned that hierarchy breaking down as everyone in the firm became empowered to improve client service.

As it turned out, I was correct. Lawyers may play a large part of the conversation when it comes to the legalities of a file, but when it comes to the process, it was made clear to me that Hunoval Law operates like a team. Everyone at the firm was trying to make things run better and smoother. And, as Cara Clausen pointed out to me, "Our teams are not afraid to butt heads with the attorneys in moving a process forward and making it better. It's very, very different from other firms."

Everyone likes to receive awards. And no organization likes receiving awards more than law firms. But what's different about Hunoval Law is that it wins awards designed for "regular" industries—awards in which no other law firms have submitted an entry. How much more impressive is it for clients, when a law firm wins awards in categories in which its own clients may be competing! But even more impressive is the ability to track and measure what these Green Belt projects have achieved for the firm, and by extension, for Hunoval Law's clients. Matt's internal calculations have shown very impressive results. In one case, the process improvements implemented by the firm's growing army of Lean Six Sigma Green Belts saved clients more than USD$4.0 million over one 18-month span.

Even in less process-driven areas of the Hunoval Law, such as bankruptcy litigation, Lean Six Sigma excitement has begun to grip the teams. Typically most litigation lawyers tell me that each case is unique and therefore, any kind of process improvement or system "just doesn't work." That statement is usually followed by a look of derision that takes pity on my stupidity. Yet, the litigation lawyers at Hunoval Law are still seeking their Green Belts. As one litigator told me, "Part of the value of Lean Six Sigma is self-critical analysis. It helps us figure out how we can do it better next time. That helps litigation because we can then separate the unique aspects of a case from the ones that happen most of the time, then build efficiencies around those aspects that happen repeatedly. We're constantly determining how the rubber meets the road. Do we *really* need *that* in the process? And better self-critical analysis definitely helps with budgeting a case. But the beautiful effect of a properly implemented system is that everyone's thinking about what's going on, and everyone is critical about what we're doing; there's constant feedback from all levels of the firm. These attributes benefit any practice area and any business model, and Lean Six Sigma is just a good way to ingrain it into our culture."

There will be litigation lawyers who point out that acting more efficiently hurts them in the pocketbook. But the other side of the coin is that efficient lawyers who close more cases should theoretically get more cases and those lawyers will simply charge for their work in a different way. As one litigator told me, "It's just a pricing dynamic."

Most other areas of Hunoval Law are already "off the clock." No one is counting hours to determine if someone is doing a good or bad job. As a result, new metrics had to be created. Cameron Scott, the firm's foreclosure managing attorney, explained, "I'm judged by timelines and reductions in errors. 'Are we moving the process along? Are we getting our orders signed? Why or why not?' We look at what the milestones are in each case so we can track and review them and turn that into a measurable. I shouldn't get beat in court if my papers are correct and on time—and I don't like to get beat in court. So, that's a pretty important metric. But it's a continual process. We need to be on the cutting edge every day to ensure we don't get beat out by the next wave."

"And the rest of your team?" I asked.

"Not that dissimilar. We track ownership of files and of the process, and that can be tied to bonuses. We use timelines a great deal," Cameron said. "So, we might determine that the fastest possible timeline for a certain matter is ten days. We can then establish a baseline and track timelines for our team. We have some monetary incentives as well as grab bags, some employee-nominated stuff, departmental pizza days and the like. But we're still a work-in-progress."

I walked back into Matt Hunoval's office. It seemed to me that the natural extension of carefully monitoring and managing your processes over thousands of files would give the firm the same treasure-trove of data that Karl Chapman was mining at Riverview Law. I wondered what Matt was doing with all his data.

"Let me take that a step further," Matt said with a smile. "Over time, because of the data that we collect, we have the opportunity to act as a *de facto* outside process improvement consultant for our clients. That is the key value-add above all else: we're not just another law firm, we're an organization that can help improve our clients' fundamental business operations. Not just a cost centre, but a business that is a cost-saver and revenue generator. That's the secret sauce." He paused. "Some of our clients collect good data on their processes, but they don't always collect the type of data that we collect. In fact, in some cases we have more data than our clients. This allows us to gain insight into what's happening within the client. We no longer have to rely upon anecdotal statements and gut-feel. We can make a clear business case and we can say, 'based on the data we've collected over the last 12 months and over 1,200 files, your failure rate is 18 percent on this particular process. Your cost of capital is $25 per day per file. And when you fail in this particular process, we have to start over; and based on the data we've collected and the analysis we've done, we've calculated that this error is costing you $1,500,000 per year.' That error has nothing to do with what we're doing as a law firm. 'So, let us help you run your shop better.' We can also offer benchmarks to clients based on how long it's taken our other clients to do the same work." *That* is powerful stuff, I thought, when a law firm can advise its clients not just on legal points but also on the fundamentals of their business. And the better Hunoval Law gets at its job, the better able the firm is to give clients a window into their own processes and efficiencies. Before "innovation" became the buzzword *du jour* in legal circles, "value-add" was all the rage: a magical ingredient that all law firms talked about in their marketing brochures, but that rarely materialized. However, Hunoval Law's strategic decision to transform into an efficient, process-driven team has turned "value-add" into an everyday occurrence.

Like most firms I visited for this book, many of the Hunoval team pointed out to me that the firm was still at the beginning of its journey. "It's a process to be the best," Matt said. "We're still on the road. But no firm is more singularly focused on streamlining processes, on making them better, and driving client results."

I looked at my watch. It was getting very late in the day and I wanted to be back in Atlanta before midnight. But I also wanted some final thoughts on what Matt had found from the journey along which he had taken his firm. Was there anything that had surprised him? Any unforeseen results?

"We saw three important benefits by going down this road. The first, most obvious, and foreseeable were the operational benefits—time saved, efficiency gains, greater visibility into our processes at both a macro- and micro-level, and fewer errors. Better for the firm, better for clients. A true win-win." He leaned back in his chair.

"The second benefit, which was unforeseen when we started, is that our people now take more *ownership* in their work. There is a 'rally around the flag' mentality or esprit de corps that comes along with doing something that no one else is doing. We're leading the field and our people can see that. We're able to attract better, more engaged people and our employee turnover is demonstrably lower than any of our competitors. And our Lean Six Sigma training gives everyone here a chance to improve their work and themselves. That's a very empowering and attractive professional development tool that no one else offers. It's something that they can take with them wherever they go—if they decide to leave.

"The third, and again unforeseen, benefit is the impact it's had on marketing and client development. A large part of our client base is comprised of Fortune 500 financial institutions, many of whom have been using variations of Lean Six Sigma for decades." Matt paused before choosing his next words. "A lot of our larger institutional clients see lawyers as Don Quixote figures—tilting at windmills but not quite getting it. Then all of a sudden we come in and we're speaking the same language. There's this 'Wow, this lawyer really *gets* it!' reaction."

Matt gave me a concrete example. He and his team had gone to a potential client's office for a pitch and they noticed Six Sigma certificates on many of the employee cubicles. The CEO was an engineer and had a lot of his staff certified. Hunoval Law was the only law firm pitching for work that was doing Six Sigma from top to bottom. Instantly, Lean Six Sigma became the key differentiator for that client. It has become a huge competitive advantage for Hunoval Law, allowing the firm to capture swaths of market share from its competitors—even in down markets. It seems that clients are even more impressed with a firm that can speak the same language as they do.

"But if it's such a huge differentiator, why haven't other law firms copied you?" I asked. It seemed like the obvious thing to do, copy success.

His response was blunt. "There's no motivation to create transformational change at traditional law firms, especially older ones. Even if they understood what we're doing, they wouldn't do it. There's a cognitive disconnect between seeing that this could work and being willing to go through the process of actually doing it. It's no different than any exercise regime you see advertised on late-night TV as you're gulping down a pint of ice cream or a pack of Doritos. You see that infomercial, pick up the phone, and order it. When it arrives at your door a few days later, it goes up on the bookshelf, unopened. And there you are the next night, gulping down yet another pint of ice cream or pack of Doritos. There needs to be total commitment—and if there isn't, nothing happens."

"And how do you keep it going?" I asked. "I mean, after you're gone?"

"I'm only 42!" he exclaimed. "But succession is something that I'm now starting to put my mind to. But really, the secret is not me. The secret is embedding this transformative idea, Lean Six Sigma, into the culture of the firm. If I can do that, the firm will last longer than me or anyone else. That's what keeps me motivated and gets me up each day. The drive for innovation and change; the challenge of embedding or institutionalizing a disruptive idea that may change the entire legal industry. That's the internal fire that keeps me going. It's the power of the idea."

Epilogue

One of the challenges of writing about the Great Legal Reformation in real time is the speed at which things change; the story of Slaters is a prime example. Unfortunately, Hunoval Law's promising story also lacks a happy ending, but for different reasons. It's trite to say that the economic conditions of 2009, when Hunoval Law began, are far different from those of 2017. When Hunoval Law was created, about 5 percent of all mortgages in the United States were going into default every year. By early 2017, those annual default rates had plummeted to historic lows of about 0.6 to 0.7 percent. This drop in default rates, combined with historic lows in US home ownership, meant that law firms whose revenues were heavily dependent upon mortgage default work became financially stretched, leading to significant market consolidation among them; others simply closed their doors.

If Hunoval Law had operated in an enlightened jurisdiction that permitted those without a law degree to invest in law firms, Matt would have had greater opportunities to seek out new capital to increase his geographic footprint to gain further economies of scale and further revenue; after all, he had a proven and successful operational model. But like so many other law firms in the United States, Hunoval Law didn't operate in such a forward-thinking jurisdiction; North Carolina forbids non-lawyers from having an ownership interest in law firms. The firm's explosive initial growth had been funded solely through operating revenue and traditional bank financing, neither of which was feasible in a soft market. That left Matt with only one option: combine with another law firm and hope to create a true case of "1+1=3."

In March, 2017 a proposed "merger of equals," Hunoval Law with BP Law Group, was announced, giving Matt the larger geographic footprint he craved. But any excitement he felt was to be short-lived. By late June 2017, the merger had fallen through and Hunoval Law had run out of cash flow and loans to keep itself afloat; Hunoval was forced to lay off the firm's entire default staff, leaving the firm with only six employees. Ironically, the antiquated regulations that keep "non-lawyers" out of American law firm ownership, also limit the ability of American law firms to seek the additional capital needed to keep their doors open and save dozens of jobs.

As of August 1, 2017, Matt had put his building up for sale, and he was pivoting his strategy to focus on real estate transactions and mortgage origination work, where Lean Six Sigma will continue to play an important part. He proudly told me that Hunoval Law became, in May 2017, the first US law firm to complete an eClosing (no paper, with all transactional documents signed by digital signatures and eNotarizations)—an area in which he wants to continue to be a pioneer.

"Looking back at applying Lean Six Sigma to legal services," he said to me during a very sombre phone call in July 2017, "I wanted to be part of something that could change our industry. Hopefully I'm a small footnote in that." He took a deep breath. "So now we start over. And that's all right." Another pause. "And who knows what the next couple years will hold? We're still at the tip of the spear in driving innovation and we're looking far ahead of the curve for the next opportunity."

Impressions

Despite its recent troubles, Hunoval Law is another illustration of the advantage that new players have in the Great Legal Reformation: a fresh, new entity, with a lean management structure, free from historical baggage, able to create and implement new strategies quickly and effectively. Matt Hunoval recognized the competitive advantage of a more efficient, process-driven approach to the firm's areas of expertise to provide faster, more accurate service to clients. Furthermore, in an era when clients demand that their service providers "understand their business," the Hunoval Law story also illustrates how law firms can gain from "speaking the same language" as their clients.

While the Hunoval Law story provides a guide to implementing process improvement techniques in a law firm, there is also a philosophical element to this story that should not be ignored.

The so-called Power of the Idea is more than just words. It's a way of thinking and approaching the business: something that permeated every aspect of Hunoval Law by giving employees the autonomy to influence how they approach their work. Hunoval Law's adoption of Lean Six Sigma also created a virtuous circle. Lean Six Sigma started out as a way to improve efficiencies and reduce errors by empowering and skilling up employees. But the more empowering Matt made his law firm, the more attractive the firm became to the best people, which improved his services, which made clients happier, which resulted in more work. None of these outcomes were based upon paying employees more money than the law firm down the street. It's a simple and effective idea that many law firms across the world have failed to grasp.

Nonetheless, the story of Hunoval Law is also a cautionary tale that, no matter how adaptive a firm may be to the Great Legal Reformation, its business strategy must also cope with macro-economic issues, particularly if a firm relies heavily upon one business sector or one practice type. No amount of Lean Six Sigma will help if the work simply dries up.

Finally, some readers may suggest that a Lean Six Sigma approach to legal services only applies in a "mill" or in a small firm environment: that it has no application in a large law firm with diverse practice areas. Those skeptics should read the next chapter.

CHAPTER 7
SEYFARTH SHAW

Lean Redux

There are many times of the year when the city of Chicago is among the most beautiful, engaging, and interesting places around which to wander: the quaintness of Andersonville in the north; an architecture river cruise through the heart of the Loop; window-shopping along the Magnificent Mile; catching a game at Wrigley Field.

November, however, is not one of those times.

Yet here I was, more than 500 miles northwest of much warmer Charlotte, looking at a Matt Hunoval-type of transformation, but this time in a mammoth legal services entity. Seyfarth (pronounced "Sigh-Farth") Shaw, or Seyfarth, as it's commonly called, is a full service firm of over 800 lawyers spread across the United States and other parts of the world. Despite its full-service moniker, the firm is particularly well-known for labour and employment law—and to the American legal press, it's become the poster child for Lean Six Sigma in a big law firm context.

Transforming a large firm such as Seyfarth from a traditional "the file will take as long as the file takes" law firm into a process-driven entity where every action on a file needs to add value, is a massive, long-term endeavour. Its journey of reformation therefore provides some good insight for large law firms. Like most large firms, rank-and-file partners have delegated a great deal of decision-making authority to a managing partner and to the firm's executive committee, giving them a relatively high degree of authority to move the firm in a preferred direction—if they have the energy, drive, and patience to do so. However, even with strong management direction, partners and associates in large firms still need to be gently and constantly nudged along a path of transformation. Partner-resistance in an industry where lateral movement between law firms is common remains a serious hurdle; unhappy partners often take themselves, their clients, and even their teams across the street to a competitor with little effort. I had had several discussions with managing partners at firms who privately expressed fear that if significant change was instituted they would not have a firm left to manage, so they defaulted to simply "keeping the ship afloat" during their management term.

If Seyfarth's long-time managing partner (and since 2016, chairman emeritus), Stephen Poor, had those fears he didn't reveal them to me. Even when I asked him the very pointed question, "How do you turn such a large ship in a new direction—without sinking it?"

He took a breath, adjusted his tall frame (one that I imagined could have made him a good point guard in his youth) then recounted the firm's journey, emphasizing to me that the process of change is indeed a long trek. In the golden years of American legal practice—the ones leading up to 2008—American law firms were exceptionally profitable; many firms saw profits increase by double digits year after year. While lawyers running those firms were slapping each other on the back, celebrating how they were doing everything correctly, it all seemed to be going just a little *too* well for Stephen. He refused to believe that past success was a positive indicator of future success. He had a nagging feeling that law firms were living in a distorted reality, and that distortion was reinforcing bad models and bad behaviour.

"The underlying economics of those stellar profits," he told me, "were based simply on increasing hourly rates. If firms wanted profits to go up by ten percent, they increased hourly rates by 14 percent; four percent covers expense increases and ten percent goes straight to the bottom line." Stephen couldn't understand how that was a sustainable business model. "Every other business in the world has to get better, stronger, faster, and cheaper; they need to add higher levels of value for their customers. Legal services, however, seemed to be immune to this economic reality."

This economic disconnect nagged at Stephen so much that he began actively looking at ways in which Seyfarth could become stronger, faster, and yes, even less expensive for clients. Just a few years before Matt Hunoval's lightbulb moment, Stephen also came to the conclusion that Lean Six Sigma could work well in a law firm. But he also knew that his vision for the firm would have to slowly play out over time, and he would have to expend significant effort to understand the psychology of the people whose behaviour he wanted to change. It had to be made clear to all Seyfarth team members not just why change was important, but what that change would entail, and that the benefits of making the change clearly outweighed its costs. Ultimately Stephen sought to encode Lean Six Sigma philosophy—what would later be called Seyfarth Lean—into the DNA of the firm, making it a way of thinking and a way of approaching the business.

With those thoughts in mind, Seyfarth began its transformation into Lean Six Sigma in 2006, facilitated by the firm's then-fledgling six-member Legal Project Management (LPM) team. Lean Six Sigma consultants were hired to come in and provide Green Belt training to the firm's executive committee, department heads, team leaders and the LPM team. Like Hunoval Law, Seyfarth quickly saw that most Lean Six Sigma tools and jargon were either unnecessary or too complex for a law firm. "We took those parts from Lean and from Six Sigma that worked best in a law firm," said Stephen, "and created our own version called Seyfarth Lean." Soon the LPM-turned-Seyfarth Lean team started a series of small projects, "undercover, no big announcement, and no asking for millions of dollars," Stephen recalled. "It took six to eight months to get our legs under us. We didn't try to boil the ocean. We didn't try to change everyone all at once."

The team intentionally chose safe internal projects that were not "owned" by any particular person, which meant they didn't step on anyone's toes. The projects also involved things that the firm had already acknowledged needed to be fixed: projects that, if improved, would directly impact all lawyers across the firm, like the firm's conflict management system. Seyfarth lawyers had been complaining about the length of time required to undertake conflicts checks, and also about the high error rates from those checks. When the system was improved as the outcome of a Seyfarth Lean project, every lawyer using the system immediately saw and understood the improvement. Seyfarth Lean was also tested with a client that gave the firm a large volume of lending work; that project increased productivity, reduced errors, and increased client satisfaction.

As part of Stephen Poor's change management strategy, successes were always shared with the firm. In fact, Stephen minced few words in early partner meetings. "You may not feel it because, like every other firm, we're doing better and better every year. But there will come a point in time where clients will be looking for higher value. We've demonstrated that we can improve our conflicts systems and our lending program, and we're going to build on that over time. We're rethinking the way we approach our business and we're not going to stop talking about this."

While early successes were crucial to moving Seyfarth Lean through the firm, it was only one piece of Stephen's strategy. "We had a number of external speakers come in and explain to the firm why we needed to change," he said. "Some of those speakers were industry experts and some came from our own clients." Stephen felt that it was vital that everyone at the firm understand that this was not a passing fad. "This was a fundamental component of who we are, what we needed to become, and what we can achieve."

However, in a firm of Seyfarth's size, a managing partner can only do so much. So it was particularly important for there to be a trusted lieutenant, or champion, who was "on the ground." Someone who would be the day-to-day face of Seyfarth Lean, continually pushing it among the firm's lawyers. Stephen was fortunate to find that champion in Lisa Damon, "a dynamic whirlwind" of a partner in Seyfarth's Boston office. Seyfarth personnel often cited Lisa and Stephen as a good "yin and yang," and both were key to the firm's success in these initiatives.

Despite the early successes, and despite the visibility and attention given to the program by top leadership, and despite being carried through the firm by Lisa Damon, for the first few years, Seyfarth Lean was still seen as an outlier by many lawyers in the firm. After all, clients were still willing to pay ever-increasing hourly billing rates. It seemed that, as long as times remained good and the firm remained very profitable, Seyfarth Lean would languish.

But the golden years of any industry never last forever. The financial crisis of 2008, in conjunction with the Association of Corporate Counsel's 2008 Value Challenge, were strong signals that the market for legal work was no longer secure. "We were dealing with scared people," Stephen said, "which allowed us to accelerate Seyfarth Lean." Seyfarth's process-driven approach worked well in helping facilitate alternative fee arrangements (AFAs) that corporate clients were then beginning to demand more often. AFAs force a law firm to jettison the billable-hours approach and assume some, or all, of the risk of inefficient service delivery.

The most legendary example of Seyfarth Lean and AFAs involved work the firm did for Wolverine World Wide. I have known Wolverine's former general counsel, Ken Grady, for many years, and it was not at all difficult to coax the story out of him: a story that he had recounted many times, and likely with the same joyful gleam in his eyes. Like many companies at the time of the 2008 financial crisis, Wolverine faced the "more for less" challenge: how can more work be done at lower cost while maintaining quality? Its legal department was not immune to this challenge, so Ken went in search of a law firm that could more efficiently manage the company's trademark portfolio of about 4,000 trademarks.

Ken himself was a believer in Lean and had, prior to joining Wolverine, received Lean training in Japan through the famed consulting firm Shingijutsu. He had also studied under Yoshiki Iwata and Senji Niwa, two members of the original Toyota Autonomous Study Group founded by Taiichi Ohno, one of the creators of the Toyota Production System. In other words, Ken was a true Lean heavyweight. Needless to say, when he heard about Seyfarth Lean he was intrigued enough to give the firm a shot at Wolverine's trademark work. "We started with a fixed annual fee which was 85 percent of the legal fees we had paid in the previous year," Ken remembered. And to make things even more challenging for Seyfarth, Wolverine's portfolio had grown larger than the year previous. In order to make any profit, Seyfarth would have to ensure it had the right people working on the file and the right processes in place.

However, Ken's goal went beyond simply reducing costs; he also saw the Seyfarth experiment as a way to improve Wolverine's own internal processes. If he could realize internal improvements he would create even further cost savings for Wolverine, as well as better managing the workload for Wolverine personnel. And, if Seyfarth contributed to those internal improvements, Ken was willing to share some of those savings with Seyfarth as a bonus, so he set about creating a number of objective metrics connected to the improvements he wanted to achieve.

The first year was such a success for both Wolverine and Seyfarth, that Ken renewed the engagement for another year—at a fixed fee that was 85 percent of the previous fee! And still the Wolverine portfolio of trademarks continued to grow. Again, a bonus structure was put into place based on what other internal improvements Ken wanted to achieve that year.

"Obviously, we couldn't do that forever," he acknowledged. "But eventually you get to the point where you feel the process is streamlined as much as possible and that the fees for the portfolio are aligned with value; whereas before, fees were aligned with effort."

As Seyfarth worked to make the trademark application workflow simpler, it discarded unneeded or duplicate steps, which not only shortened the timeline for the entire process, but also dramatically improved the quality of Wolverine's trademark applications. Prior to using Seyfarth, only about 25 percent of Wolverine's applications for a new trademark were approved on initial application; 75 percent were sent back for further amendment by government officials. This seemed to be consistent with the industry average for new trademark applications and so it was seen as simply "the way things are." But with a redesigned process that approval rate was flipped on its head; 75 percent of Wolverine's initial applications for a new trademark were approved, while only 25 percent were sent back for amendment. The entire process had truly become better, faster, cheaper. It was little wonder then, that the silver-haired Ken Grady was, for a few years, Seyfarth's Lean Law evangelist and now teaches Lean at Michigan State University Law School's exceptional LegalRnD program.

"Most lawyers make the mistake of thinking that Lean is simply a cost-cutting measure," Ken told me. "Lean is a philosophy through which we look at value from the client's perspective and focus what we do on delivering that value while respecting people."[20] He gave me the example of a lawyer sending a well-crafted memo to her client only to receive the response, "Thanks, but that memo didn't really help me." The lawyer may have provided insightful legal analysis, but in Lean philosophy, since the memo was not helpful to the client *from the client's perspective*, the lawyer simply created waste. Further, if value from the client's perspective is delivered in a way that disrespects people, the lawyer has not been true to Lean philosophy. Ken gave me the example of a law firm that forces its teams to do otherwise automatable tasks, 12 hours a day, in order to deliver value to clients. Asking teams to do those tasks without considering alternative methods, or without asking for input from the teams on how to improve, is disrespectful to the teams and is not Lean thinking. In short,

---

[20]   This quote and the following discussion of Lean philosophy is taken from Ken Grady's insightful blog post. See Ken Grady, "Lean is not about Cost Cutting," *LinkedIn* (May 4, 2015): https://www.linkedin.com/pulse/lean-cost-cutting-kenneth-grady.

while every process improvement exercise will ultimately seek to eliminate certain steps, that elimination is not simply for the purpose of cutting costs. Eliminating waste provides value to the client from the client's perspective and shows respect for those using the process, something that Hunoval Law saw in spades. The real question, however, was: could something similar happen in a large-firm context?

At the time I visited their offices, the Seyfarth Lean numbers being bandied about were very impressive. "We've seen 10 to 20 percent reductions in the amount of hours our lawyers spend on some files," Kim Craig, managing director of the firm's Lean Solutions group told me. We were sitting in one of the firm's boardrooms fitted out with all manner of technology. Her face, framed by locks of long reddish-brown hair, beamed as we talked. "We've changed the resource allocations on files and improved cycle times. We've done well over 500 legal process maps and touched every department and every practice group of the firm."

Kim's excitement was contagious, but I wondered how much of Seyfarth Lean philosophy had actually permeated the firm. "Are 100 percent of attorneys working in entirely new ways? No," she replied. "Some have changed radically—some only moderately—but the entire firm is now thinking differently and that's part of the journey."

Client-Facing Teams Who Didn't Go to Law School

Most exciting to me was when Kim recounted the growing value of non-legally trained, client-facing personnel. To have anyone who was not a lawyer deal directly with a client is virtually unheard of in legal services. The hierarchy is clear: the partner owns the client; associates may have limited client contact under the strict understanding that the partner must know about that interaction and make all decisions regarding that client; and those without legal training are permitted to have client interaction for the purposes of arranging deliveries or lunches.

Consistent with Lean philosophy, Kim's group works directly with clients so the group can understand what clients see as valuable and then design solutions from the client's perspective rather than the firm's perspective. "Other firms focus exclusively on what the lawyer needs—whether it's knowledge management, technology, legal project management, or process improvement. Those groups have a service role, but in service to the lawyers," Kim told me. "We've reversed that here. Our group focuses on the client, and works in service of the client."

As the non-legally trained team members became client-facing, it soon became clear that technology would have a huge role in creating solutions for clients. "This meant that we needed to hire legal technologists, not traditional IT support thinkers," Kim said. "We wanted business partners who would meet with clients and attorneys. And as a result, we now think about our world in terms of 'services design,' which has created some emerging non-traditional roles in the firm—such as legal solutions architects (technologists who happen to be attorneys) who pair with project managers and attorneys to figure out what technical underpinnings we need to put into place to help make this work effectively."

One of the newest roles in the Lean Solutions group is that of data solutions architect: a person who determines the type of data the firm should be collecting on files, how it's to be done, and the type of reports that the firm should be making to clients. These reports go beyond typical financial data. The goal is to unpack analytics about the law practice to better understand what Seyfarth is doing and how Seyfarth is doing it. "It also helps make prognostications on how cases will play out." It's not surprising then that Seyfarth is a data fiend. "We don't track data just to track it," Kim told me. "We're tracking data because we can use it to build documents, or so we can filter it, or slice and dice it for enhanced awareness and insight: both for the firm and for the client. Collecting the right data also allows us to create metrics for clients. We sit down with the client to determine how the client is assessed and the types of reports the client needs, then we build it. We may also have service-level agreements tied to certain things, so we also need that data."

Unsurprisingly, Lean Solutions was, at the time I visited, one of the fastest growing departments of the firm. "We have the largest group of client-facing client managers in the industry, and our team has grown to 35 in LPM and Technology, with over ten pure software engineers and developers who push out code every Sunday." The firm is also attracting non-law graduates from the University of Chicago and from Northwestern University. "We're doing something different. People are excited about coming to work and doing something they're passionate about."

The growth and importance of the Lean Solutions group can also be seen from the growing chorus of requests from Seyfarth clients who liked what Seyfarth was doing with technology and process, and who want to use those items in-house. As a result, Seyfarth Lean Consulting, a standalone entity, was created to advise companies (not law firms) seeking ways to make themselves more operationally effective.

Legal Expertise as Merely Table Stakes

Having seen what's happening at Seyfarth, I began to consider that quality legal expertise is fast becoming nothing more than table stakes. It gets a firm in the door, but it doesn't necessarily mean that the work will be won. "Clients know our lawyers are good, but clients also care about *how* we're going to do the legal work," Kim said. When it comes to client "pitches," where law firms trot out their superstar lawyers to woo work from new clients, Seyfarth will send a legal project manager, a legal solutions architect, and perhaps a data analyst, in addition to its lawyers. "The Lean Solutions team members are there to describe how we're going to execute, how we came up with the budget, and how we determined staffing. We often provide a process map that reflects all this thinking," she said. While this provides added value at client presentations and helps win work, it also allows the capture of a greater range of "pitch" expertise and client intelligence for Seyfarth as an entity: tacit knowledge that at traditional firms would remain only in the heads of those lawyers who actually took part in those pitches. The average Seyfarth partner may be part of only five or six client pitches a year, while the Lean Solutions team averages about 75 pitches per year; and all knowledge from those 75 pitches is able to be systematically captured, used, and distributed.

Sticky Clients Make For Sticky Lawyers

Seyfarth's gradual adoption of Seyfarth Lean, as a mentality and as a philosophy, also seems to be creating an enterprise approach to legal services delivery within the firm. Often Kim and her team are asked to meet with lawyers who are considering a move to Seyfarth, many of whom have existing practices and are searching for a firm with the best platform for them to succeed. A platform that will augment their expertise and create differentiation in the marketplace. It is not uncommon for these lateral hires to comment, "This platform allows me to do things that I couldn't do elsewhere."

"That's a double-edged sword," I pointed out. "If laterals are moving because they can't do these things at other firms, they won't be able to leave Seyfarth very easily, either—they could never go back to practicing law at a more traditional firm."

Kim smiled. "We don't have any data on that," she said coyly. "But I can't think of any partners we work with regularly, who have recently left for other firms."

I deliberately made no response, staring at her with a smile that said, "Come on, just between you and me, what's the real answer?" Whether she got weirded out by my smile or she folded under the pressure, she finally blurted out, "And, yes, it does make a lawyer's practice less portable."

Client stickiness is often reinforced at firm events where clients have been very candid about why they chose Seyfarth. It's not unusual for clients to say, "But for the technology and process improvement, we would have gone elsewhere." In fact, Kim told me that clients have delayed assignments until all process team members were available, notwithstanding that the lawyers were ready to go. "We've become that highly valued by clients."

There are limits to a "lawyers only" approach. The real magic happens when you intertwine the lawyers with technology and process teams. "Our team can't do the legal work, and the lawyers can't do the tech or process piece; we each need each other, "Kim said. "So while the old traditional lines between 'lawyer' and 'non-lawyer' have not completely eroded here, it's moving in that direction. It's the end of the practice of law as we know it—an entirely new ballgame."

Impressions

Seyfarth Shaw presents the classic management challenge for all large law firms: moving hundreds of lawyers in a new and completely different direction. While some luck was involved, through the financial crisis and changing client demands, the decision to seek competitive advantage in process improvement still needed firm, committed leadership with the stamina to continue along that path despite missteps and despite any dissension from partners. The Seyfarth saga suggests that successful change in a large firm comes from the top down, not from the bottom up, and that it requires leadership that continually walks the talk. However, that leadership also needs someone in the trenches, carrying the torch day in and day out.

Seyfarth's journey also illustrates the benefit of investing in small inexpensive pilot projects that don't step on partners' sensitive toes, and that avoid boiling the ocean. This creates early wins that build momentum and showcase the benefits of change. Like Hunoval Law, a new Seyfarth Lean philosophy resulted in unintended, but welcome, changes in firm dynamics that, if continued, will completely transform Seyfarth over time. Furthermore, echos of Riverview Law also reverberate through the Seyfarth story: Seyfarth understood the importance of data analytics and the opportunity to create a consulting arm; in addition, the Seyfarth Lean philosophy made clients loyal and sticky to the entity rather than to individual lawyers.

The key however, will be continuation. With Stephen Poor moving to chairman emeritus in 2016, and Ken Grady and others departing thereafter, the question of sustainability has to be raised. What effect, if any, will this have on Seyfarth Lean? Will Seyfarth continue with this philosophy, or will it settle back into the traditional ways of practice? Will Seyfarth end up being a cautionary tale of how easy it is to lose gains? One certainly hopes not, but only time will answer those questions.

Nonetheless, readers should clearly take away from the discussions in this chapter, and in the previous one, that a philosophy of continuous improvement, whether it's called Lean or Lean Six Sigma or Seyfarth Lean, is not a "one and done" initiative. Process improvement never ends; it needs to be continually nurtured and incorporated into the psyche of employees by strong champions throughout the firm—especially at the highest levels.

CHAPTER 8

VALOREM LAW GROUP

"And Now for Something Completely Different"

Despite only coming into vogue after World War Two, the billable hour has been thoughtlessly used as the *only* metric for pricing legal services. However useful it may have been for lawyers in the past, the days of the billable hour may be numbered for many areas of practice where clients are demanding price certainty based upon value received, not effort expended. Careful readers will have already noticed a subtle shift away from billable hour pricing by entities discussed in previous chapters. This chapter provides illumination on one firm that has unshackled itself from the billable hour in an area of law where practitioners have consistently stated that the billable hour must be used: litigation.

While in Chicago meeting with personnel at Seyfarth Shaw, I shivered across town for a short visit to the offices of Valorem Law Group. On its face, Valorem looks like just another boutique practice specializing in commercial litigation. At the time I visited, it was a partnership populated by four equity partners, three non-equity partners, and three associates. It didn't have a crew of IT professionals attempting to make it technologically advanced; it didn't have teams of other professionals driving process, nor did it have a radical decision-making structure. In many ways, it gave the appearance of a traditional law firm.

But while touring the office, I began to find snippets of what made this firm different from its competitors. Its library was heavily populated with business books, rather than legal books; its walls were covered with philosophical statements about the importance of the client, and of being different—all of which fed into the unique pricing philosophy that had brought me here in the first place.

Many lawyers across the world cling tightly to the concept of pricing their services by the hour, and clients often view a higher rate per hour as a proxy for quality: the higher a lawyer's hourly rate, the better she must be. However, there has been a growing movement away from billable hours and toward value pricing.[21] In the United States, Valorem is recognized as a leader of value pricing in a litigation practice,[22] something that many litigators across the world dismiss as impossible. I therefore wanted to see it for myself.

Valorem's founder, Patrick Lamb, bounded into the firm's boardroom (affectionately known as the "Bored Room" by his team) casually dressed, and sporting a salt-and-red-pepper goatee. The room was filled with awards and client compliments. One of these caught my eye: an 8 × 10 inch framed photo of Superman flying across the sky holding a sign that read, "Hot Wash." Superman's face was replaced with the face of Jeff Carr, former General Counsel of FMC Technologies, who was a client

---

[21] See Ronald Baker, *Implementing Value Pricing: A Radical Business Model for Professional Firms* (Wiley, 2010). See also Ron Baker, "Timesheets are Terrible Cost Accountants," *VerSage Institute* (May 23, 2011): http://www.verasage.com/blog/timesheets-are-terrible-cost-accountants/.

[22] See also Patrick Lamb, *Alternative Fees for Litigators and their Clients* (American Bar Association, 2014) and Patrick Lamb, *Alternative Fee Arrangements: Value Fees and the Changing Legal Market* (Ark Publishing, 2010).

of Valorem. In the bottom left corner were the letters WWW (short for: what went well), while at the bottom right corner were the letters TALA (short for: take a look at).

Patrick saw my puzzled look. "A hot wash, or after action assessment, is what we do at the end of every file," he explained. "We gather the team that worked on a file and ruthlessly assess what went well and what didn't go so well. We then share that discussion with the client to get her perspective and ask her the same things: what did we do well, and what do we need to take a look at?"

"It must take a lot of courage to ask for a critique of your performance," I ventured.

"Sure, but it's also been a pretty useful tool for us. It helps ensure that we're continuously improving how we provide our services. The clients are pretty insightful, and actually, we're much harder on ourselves." He shifted in his seat, then added, "We want clients to recognize *that we recognize* when we make mistakes, and hopefully we don't make the same mistake twice. Most clients do the after action review as part of their business anyway, so this just brings what they do, normally, into our world."

Having an eye for continual improvement was sounding familiar to me.

"Our team is filled with true believers," Patrick said. "They stick around because we do interesting work and it's a fun environment—but also because we're constantly looking for new and better ways of doing things—people really like that."

"Saying 'true believers' makes it sound rather cultish," I jabbed.

He laughed. "Look, people have to be believers here. They have to believe in gauging everything we do from the perspective of the client and they have to believe in changing away from the billable hour. When it comes down to it, 'hours' is the silliest form of measurement for legal services. It doesn't tell you anything. It doesn't tell you whether the time spent on the file was good, bad or indifferent."

"But if you take away hours," I challenged him, "how can you measure performance and award compensation? After all, the metric most used to reward and advance lawyers in North American law firms is anchored around how many hours they bill."

Patrick was nonplussed.

"We do it just like our clients do it. At the beginning of each year we define our goals as a firm as well as the goals for each person in the firm. At the end of the year we measure how well a person performed relative to those goals. We look at other things as well: How are we performing on our cases? Are we getting good outcomes? Are we using creative and strong approaches? Are our team members progressing from one area to the next?"

He took a breath. "Is there still some subjectivity and mysticism to it? Sure. But we try to be as transparent as possible. Look, we're not breaking any new ground here. We're simply saying: this is how our clients deal with these issues—so it should work for us.

"I also don't believe that lawyers should be guaranteed a profit on every hour they work, and I certainly don't believe they're entitled to a 40 percent profit year in and year out. I believe that lawyers should have the price pressure of being more efficient and they should deliver outcomes more efficiently. There will always be cases where you screw up the pricing and not make much money—deal with it! Every business faces this."

I was beginning to warm up to Patrick. He was honest about his approach and I could see why clients liked him, and why it would be fun to work with him.

"There were two things that always bothered me about billing by the hour," he continued. It seems that I had revved him up. I was glad that my recorder was fully charged because he was clearly on a roll. "At my previous law firm, billing by the hour placed a cap on my earnings. And second, I hated situations where I had won a case and I knew the other guy was getting paid more than me, simply because he had a higher hourly rate. It made no sense to me. But what brought things to a head was when I received an unpleasant phone call from one of my larger clients—a conversation that I'll never forget:

> *[The client] said, 'have you seen our stock price today?' I responded that I hadn't.*
>
> *'Well, we got hammered. And do you know why we got hammered?'*
>
> *Again I responded that I didn't know.*
>
> *'We got hammered because we missed our earnings target by a penny per share. And do you know why we missed our earnings target?'*
>
> *I said that I didn't, but I was sure that he was going to tell me.*
>
> *'We missed our earnings target by almost the exact amount that your fees exceeded the budget for all our litigation.' There was then a pause on the line. 'Do you have any idea what just happened to my personal net worth?'"*

That client then worked with Patrick to create better budgets and to put caps on the fees charged on its files. Patrick said that he then became obsessed with never going over budget—it was a challenge, and a form of gamification. But most of all, he didn't want another angry phone call.

However, despite the fact that he never exceeded another budget, and in fact, he often stayed well under budget, something still didn't seem fair. The only incentive for coming in under budget was not receiving an angry phone call. And since there was no incentive to come in *well* under budget, the budget caps became targets; it meant that lawyers could game the work on a file to fit perfectly within the budget, with no need to invest in truly reworking their processes to come further under budget.

Patrick decided that his pricing needed to be further tweaked in order to create the right results: value for money for clients as well as an incentive for the lawyer to maximize profit margins by working more efficiently—just like in every other industry.

He went to his firm at that time, and suggested pricing reform. Much like Stephen Poor across town, Patrick was convinced that the traditional practice of lawyers annually raising their hourly rates by eight percent, nine percent or ten percent was not sustainable. At some point clients would say "enough is enough." However, those suggestions fell on deaf ears. In fact, "no one at the firm even wanted to talk about it. They thought I was insane!" Patrick remembered.

The turning point came in 2007 when Patrick happened to meet President John F. Kennedy's special advisor and speechwriter, Ted Sorenson. Upon hearing Patrick's concerns, Sorenson gave him some sage advice: "You need to decide if you want to spend energy getting your firm to move toward the space you want to be in. Or whether you want to be in the space you want to be in."

As Patrick recalled, "It was like getting hit in the head with a two-by-four. I told Sorenson, 'I hate when you old guys say stuff like that! You make it sound so simple.' But he was exactly right. Some people like the process, and some people don't. A year later I started Valorem."

When Patrick and his colleagues started Valorem in 2008, his vision was to design a law firm built around what was best for the client and one that would foster equality and teamwork: every equity partner would always be paid the same amount of money since every equity partner brought something important to the firm. "We don't need to argue about pay," he said. "There's no 'what's in it for me' attitude because a rising tide raises all boats."

Ideally, Patrick told me, he wants a diamond-shaped firm: a few equity partners at the top, a big middle of people to run cases day-to-day, and a few younger lawyers at the bottom to organically grow into the firm. Such a model keeps firm management nimble and provides enough scale to do a wide range of work. Such a model also raises a set of new challenges: such as how to incent and keep those who are not equity partners engaged and happy for long careers, something that Valorem will have to eventually contend with. However, Valorem doesn't want to be a massive legal juggernaut. "In many ways, growth is a perception issue for us. Clients want us to have a sufficient bench to handle their matters, but beyond that our strategy is not to be huge," Patrick said.

In terms of management, Valorem's managing partner is voted in annually and makes a great many decisions without much other input. However, the closer decisions come to core values and mission-critical matters (hiring, firing, core changes), the more other partners are involved. This keeps management nimble. But the firm also has an unofficial advisory group of about nine people that Valorem uses as a sounding board for ideas or problems. The group is informal, so as to not run afoul of the rules in the United States that prevent non-lawyers from controlling, or having an ownership in, American law firms. It's a regulatory rule that Patrick calls "ridiculous." But the slight possibility of the American legal market someday allowing outside investment in law firms was a partial driver in creating the firm's name. "Valorem is a neutral name. It's not about the person, it's about a model or a way of delivering legal services. And if it comes to that, I want investors investing in a model, not a person."

The Valorem model is based on experienced lawyers, although Valorem does have some younger lawyers with less than ten years of experience. The experienced-lawyer paradigm brings immediate dividends to clients because of Valorem's approach: "keeping the end in mind" and forcing lawyers to think about what the end needs to look like in order for the client to succeed. This means that his team only looks at those issues that are going to change the outcome of the case. "Many litigators spend a great deal of time uncovering stones in a case," Patrick said. "Here's a stone, uncover it. Here's a stone, uncover it. There's no plan, or even a coherent process. We don't do that. I tell clients, 'we're not going to uncover every stone. So we won't guarantee that we'll learn everything, but we *will* learn the stuff that we need to know to try the case. We may miss something—but the cost of seeing everything is pretty expensive with little added benefit.' Most clients understand that, and are not averse to taking some risk." This more strategic, risk-assessed approach is what Patrick calls "skinnying the file." Lawyers need to be better at "skinnying the file," he told me, and only do those things that clearly advance the client's interests.

How then, does a boutique law firm handle what can sometimes be a sea of documents to review for a case—even if one is only turning over the stones that matter? How does it achieve scale? The answer is to create a strategic partnership with a trusted outside provider—in this case with Novus Law, a third-party provider that performs document review, management and analysis for lawyers. The Novus Law team is trained to look for what Valorem needs for each case.

Every case is also project-managed to some degree. In the Valorem collaboration room, I saw the 90-day run-up to trial mapped on a large white board. All steps were mapped into "swim lanes" so that the sequence and ownership of each step was clearly identified. These maps are also shared with clients, so the client knows what's going on and can make any suggested changes. Adopting a project management approach forces the team to think about every step and put them in the right sequence, far in advance. It instills rigour and discipline, and allows the team to monitor, "so that we can catch when things are behind, or going wrong."

As Patrick walked me to the bank of elevators, I realized that while Valorem may start from a different point than other firms in this book, it soon drives along the same path: one that is client-centric and focussed on self-improvement.

While we waited for the arrival of one of the office building's elevators, I asked one last question. "What else is different about Valorem? Did we miss anything?"

"Well," he said and paused, seeming unsure if he should mention what was on his mind. After a long second, he added, "I believe we're the only law firm that's done an exorcism." He laughed then explained that one of his team was feeling like she was living under a cloud. Computer problems in the office afflicted only her; she had numerous flight cancellations, hotel reservation problems, and a bad decision on a motion. She thought she was cursed. "So we decided to conduct an exorcism, gathering everybody, either in person or on Skype, into the conference room; we lit candles, and formed a circle around her while reciting chants. She soon recovered her mojo and went on to bigger and better things."

I wasn't quite sure what to say after that; and since the elevator had then arrived, I just thanked him again for his time and stepped into the elevator car, bracing myself for the journey back into the cold November winds.

Impressions

Interestingly, much of what Valorem is doing has resonance in the Lean philosophy that I had seen at Seyfarth Shaw and at Hunoval Law. Patrick had intuitively come to the same conclusion as many others in an effort to bring value to his clients. A big part of that value was working in a smarter, more efficient manner. Patrick also understood that "value" was a two-way street that created a win/win for the client and the lawyer; both had to be happy with the process and the result.

Like others in this book, Patrick could see that the old ways of practice, while lucrative, were making less and less sense. It was better to change earlier rather than later, even if that meant leaving the comfort and security of his previous firm. Moreover, Patrick is still very much a driving force at Valorem, which ensures that the philosophies around which the firm was originally built remain firmly in place. Further, Patrick's comment that Valorem is not about a person, but about a model of delivering legal services, is consistent with the entity-based approach to legal services that other firms in this book have sought. The goal is for clients to come to Valorem not for a particular person, but because of the way the entity known as Valorem delivers legal services.

What's most instructive about the Valorem experience is that it has shattered the myth of litigation pricing; billing by the hour is not the only, or even the best, way to price for this area of practice. But such an approach requires a very different mindset, forcing lawyers to: properly scope each file at the onset; fully involve clients with a strategy aimed at only doing what's necessary to achieve the agreed goal; and to accept the risk of getting the pricing wrong. None of this is radical, but it requires thoughtfulness, experience, and confidence— which are what clients value in a professional. And in return for the value received, a client will give profit to the professional.

PART THREE

A POTPOURRI OF ALTERNATIVE TRAILBLAZERS IN VIGNETTE FORM

While the cool kids of legal technology may ultimately change the way legal services are delivered over the next 25 years, lawyers already have access to enough affordable, helpful technology to create new delivery models that provide significant value to clients. The firms discussed in Part Three have seen that harnessing the power of existing technology is more than sufficient for them to gain competitive advantage through new models of service delivery.

These firms defy categorization and are founded upon an assortment of ideas united by the common theme of adapting to the Great Legal Reformation.

CHAPTER 9
gunner*cooke*
Plug and Play Platforms, Part 1

The manicured courtyards and ancient buildings of Jesus Hall at England's famed Oxford University seemed a strange place for an innovative law firm to hold a retreat. In fact, it might be seen as the antithesis of new legal service delivery systems. But if the 30 or so lawyers in attendance at gunner*cooke*'s (the lower case spelling and italics are deliberate) first firm retreat back in the autumn of 2014 felt that way, they didn't show it to me. During the lunch breaks and cocktail hours I sensed growing excitement over the fact that they were part of something that was really breaking new ground.

On the last day of the retreat I watched perhaps one of the best ever law firm leadership speeches; the lights were dimmed as an old Roger Whittaker song, *New World in the Morning*, was pumped up over the room's speakers and co-founder Darryl Cooke sashayed up to the microphone. Despite the funny performance, he asked a fundamental question.

"What happens to a decent person who is forced to work long hours at a job she doesn't like, in conditions she cannot control, for clients who don't express appreciation or even acknowledge her existence?"

He paused, watching heads nod around the room. There was an unspoken bond with the audience. We had all been there.

"When people work under conditions like this, with little time for personal life and even less time for the personal interests that they used to enjoy, they become vindictive, bitter, and not fun to be around."

More nods. On Darryl went, playing to the angst and dismay of the very experienced lawyers in the room, all of whom would be classified as generation Xers or even baby boomers, and had Malcolm Gladwell's famed 10,000 hours of experience —most also had significant in-house or business experience. There was nary a millennial in sight, except for the firm's fresh-faced support team.

Looking back, it's clear that Darryl's speech was a veiled explanation of the creation of gunner*cooke*: a firm born out of frustration with a model that no longer seemed fit for purpose. He later admitted to me that he had felt this way for many years and he had moved among some of the UK's premier law firms in constant search of greener pastures, but never found them. During those wandering years, Darryl spoke to a number of chief executive officers at large- and mid-sized companies, asking them what they disliked most about their lawyers. Their answers all seemed to be remarkably consistent: (i) having to use inexperienced, junior lawyers; (ii) uncertainty of fees; and (iii) a lack of commercial thinking. And so it was this combination of unhappiness and client research that finally culminated in Darryl making his move to create a new model firm. But he wanted a solid partner with the same vision.

Sarah Goulbourne had been general counsel at a number of large corporations and had run across Darryl in various capacities over the previous 20 years. As luck would have it, Darryl learned that Sarah was also considering a move. Since they were both in the Northwest of England, he suggested coffee just outside of Manchester, in the tiny village of Alderley Edge: the type of village where one could meet in private and not worry about competitors overhearing your vision. It was here that the two hatched a plan for a new firm that would not only address the emotional disconnect they had both seen in English law firms, but also bring joy back to the practice of law. They both loved the stimulation of legal practice, they just didn't love the way lawyers were being forced to practice it. They knew that if they got it right, they could tap into a huge vein of talent that was equally disaffected.

"But what about the name?" I asked. "It's unusual and very cool, but I don't get it."

Darryl was somewhat shy about explaining the story. "Gunner" was his father's nickname as a child and while his father wasn't a lawyer, he *was* instrumental in encouraging his son to take on the risk of a new venture—all while in his last months in a hospice for terminally ill cancer patients. "You'll never be happy until you do it," Darryl remembered his father saying. "He gave me the confidence to do it, and he was right. When he died and Sarah couldn't yet join due to work restrictions, it seemed appropriate to use his name." He paused and added, "although he never knew that we used it."

Beyond having a great name, Darryl and Sarah both understood that real competitive advantage for lawyers came from delivering legal services in a way that was different from their competitors. They knew that English firms like Riverview Law and Radiant Law were based on process, IT, and volume; but that was not a place where they wanted to compete. They wanted to create a place where very senior lawyers could work as a collective, with enhanced IT and back-office support to service mid-tier corporations. They created a hub-and-spoke model with a back office "hub" located in lower-cost Manchester, and a "spoke" in higher-priced London. The spoke in London is located in a five-star serviced office facility in the heart of the city, just steps from the Bank of England and the Royal Exchange, giving the firm all the prestige of a central London location at a fraction of the cost. Even so, many gunner*cooke* lawyers work from their home offices and mostly use the London location for client meetings. It was in the majestic common area, a domed two-storey lounge, where I once again met up with these legal rebels to see how things had progressed from the time of the 2014 retreat. Darryl, in full suit and tie, with a bit of greying, but not untidy, scruff, sat next to blonde, blue-eyed Sarah.

The early days of the firm were admittedly tough as gunner*cooke* sought to find the right lawyers for the model. "It's not for everyone," Sarah cautioned. It's also why gunner*cooke* invests heavily in a formal 90-day immersion process for new recruits to ensure that they transition well. I could well imagine the culture shock of a senior lawyer, used to having staff, students, and lawyers at her beck and call, suddenly having to manage files completely on her own in a dispersed, virtual firm environment. The pair admit that they're getting much better at spotting people who work well in the model.

"We're more discerning as to who we add as we grow," Sarah said. "You need to have strong confidence in yourself to succeed here. If you have that, you have the opportunity to get away from management structure, politics, and bureaucracy." The biggest challenges lawyers face when joining gunner*cooke* are pricing, winning work, and becoming business people. "We put vast amounts of work into this—in our development office we have a pricing consultant that works with our partners," Darryl said. "We've developed a very processed and knowledgeable approach to business development. We also have a project and client management consultant in the development office, because we believe that the quality of service we and our clients demand goes way beyond technical ability." It was clear to me that gunner*cooke* was searching for, and building, the famed "T-shaped lawyer" that has been talked about in legal circles for years: a lawyer with a depth of legal skills as well as a broad range of service delivery skills, such as project management skills, Lean skills, technology skills, business skills, and the like.

They also both stressed that culture is their key to success. "Everyone can copy what we do," Darryl said. "But they can't copy our culture. We work extremely hard at making the environment work for everyone. It's the happiest place I have ever worked, by far." He paused. "We're aiming to be the best law firm in the world—not on revenues or number of offices or partners, but on client service. Every lawyer has their own NPS score and the development office works with each lawyer to improve their score."

I had to ask what a NPS score was, as I had not heard of the Net Promotor Score. Something the pair borrowed from the retail world, it's based on one simple question: *On a scale of one to ten, would you refer me to others?* That question is sent out with every client invoice. gunner*cooke* then compiles the scores for each lawyer and the development office works with each lawyer to bring up their skills. It's not used as a tool for punishment, but as an indication where training may be needed. And from a lawyer's point of view, a better NPS score should translate into higher revenue. Eventually the firm will publish a firm-wide average for public consumption.

All gunner*cooke* lawyers are independent contractors and the early days featured lawyers managing legal files that only required one or two lawyers, making the arrangement prone to siloed work arrangements with little crossover. "We're now at about 190 lawyers and growing at about 50 lawyers per year," Darryl said. "So there's no work that the firm can't support. However we still give our lawyers the flexibility to work with other law firms or other lawyers if that is what the client requests." I shook my head for a second as I wasn't sure that I had heard him correctly. I asked if he meant that gunner*cooke* lawyers could work with other law firms for the same client on the same file.

"Of course! Our goal is to give the client the best service and to put the best team together," Darryl said. "We believe it's the way of the future and the only way to keep flexibility in the model without horrendous overhead."

I wondered about fee guidelines.

"Lawyers set their own fees," Darryl said. "All that we insist upon is a fixed-fee policy to give clients budget certainty and no surprises. Our model is not about cheapness. These are senior lawyers and so they should get the market rate. We help them work through milestones and deliverables and how to charge for each. In addition, we provide an administrative structure around each lawyer, and of course they have access to our other lawyers. Our proposition to lawyers is simple: all you have to do is the fee earning and project delivery." And while no one gets paid until the outside client pays its account, "there should be no dispute about the account because you've agreed on the price in advance and so," Darryl added, "there should also be no fear to collect that account from a client."

Both Sarah and Darryl knew that one of the challenges of a dispersed firm is creating a sense of belonging. "We work hard at a social agenda to knit the lawyers together and to make them feel a part of something and to identify with it," Sarah said. "We want them to feel that this is the best place they've ever worked—that it's the greatest bit of their careers!" Darryl was quick to point out the fallacy that sharing physical space automatically creates a social connection between the people working there. "At traditional firms, many lawyers are so disengaged from how the firm is being run, that there's no emotional connection—there's just a financial connection."

"We're also a learning organization," Sarah added. "Everyone who joins understands that we're in a continuous improvement cycle. Even the back-office team."

As was my wont, I asked about the structure of the firm. Originally it seemed the firm was structured as a limited liability partnership, with just Sarah and Darryl as partners. However, they soon realized that restructuring as an alternative business structure would give them greater flexibility in attracting both shareholders and business expertise. Finance Director David Coombes soon joined and took a stake in the company.

"We're also highly focussed on good corporate governance," Sarah told me. This is unsurprising given her general counsel experience. gunner*cooke* currently has five independent board members. "We want to bring in disciplines from other businesses to help us. Our board challenges us and we need that! It's dynamic and driven, which is a big change from the executive boards or committees at most law firms." Perhaps it's the diversity of the board or the natural fearlessness of these two entrepreneurial co-founders but they both went to great lengths to tell me that failure at gunner*cooke* is nothing to be ashamed of.

"We'll try something and if it doesn't work, we don't fuss about it," Darryl said. "We're not hung up if we didn't make it work. OK, it didn't work. Move on. And we try to reinforce that thinking into a firm motto—there's no such thing as failure, the only failure is not trying. People here get criticized for not trying, but not for failing."

And gunner*cooke* certainly does its fair share of trying new things. In 2015, gunner*cooke* Consulting was born from the realization that gunner*cooke*'s clientele required not only legal advice, but also sound, ongoing business advice from senior, experienced business advisors: a consultancy practice that has now grown to 35 consultants. In 2017, the consultancy launched an operating partner offering, housing more than 25 operating partners for mid-market private equity projects.

Law students and young lawyers often bemoan the fact that opportunities in innovative and dispersed firms are often restricted to well-experienced lawyers, leaving them out in the cold and forcing them to train in traditional firms. Responding to this criticism in 2016, gunner*cooke* introduced organic growth to the model through gunner*bloom*: salaried roles for lawyers with one to five years of legal experience. "We send them on secondments and also give them general legal experience working with senior lawyers across gunner*cooke* for three years," Darryl told me. "After that, they can specialize in a specific area of law. Throughout their tenure they don't fill out any time sheets, they work with a mentor, and they receive training in pricing and business development. Our expectation is that they'll join gunner*cooke* when they reach their 10,000 hours and have enough clients—and we help them get there."

In another innovative twist, during their second or third year, gunner*bloom*ers are tasked with setting up a personal not-for-profit charity to meet a social need, working with gunner*cooke*'s charitable foundation, inspire*. And while gunner*cooke* provides administrative support for each charity, each is led by the gunner*bloom*er who created it, giving her hands-on business operations experience.

As I had heard so often in my travels, the mantra of constant evolution soon emerged, not only to keep the firm competitive, but also to keep the firm's personnel happy. "We've got to keep supporting and reinventing how we service our lawyers and keep making it better and better. We have to show that we're trying new things and innovating because the risk is that they'll say, 'what are you doing for my money?'" Sarah said. "Or they leave."

"And if we're doing this right," Darryl added, "Why would you want to leave? We want you to stay for your entire career, not just a stage of your career. You can stay and work until you're 80. Or take six months off if you want. We made gunner*cooke* to help lawyers become fulfilled. It's a place where you'll get the most out of your life."

Sarah then added, "We want to create better, happier, and more commercial lawyers."

Who could one argue with that?

Impressions

When I left gunner*cooke's* London office, there was nothing but sunshine in the forecast so I chose to take a long walk back to Notting Hill where my friend had lent me his flat. For those unfamiliar with London, it's a very long walk! But it also gave me time to think about gunner*cooke's* place in the Great Legal Reformation. In a very short time span, the firm had become a notable competitor in the English legal market by shedding itself of the overhead, bureaucracy, and politics of the old guard, making it nimble, attentive, and accessible. This was not, as Darryl Cooke pointed out, a labour arbitrage play competing on fees. Instead, gunner*cooke*'s secret sauce is deceptively simple: take away the friction points of a traditional law firm; bolster lawyer autonomy and freedom; invest in methods that make lawyers happy; actively help lawyers become successful— all fully supported by existing technology that permits optimized, flexible and dispersed operations. Given its growth trajectory, it's not inconceivable that gunner*cooke* could be the model that replaces some large law firm environments, particularly with the advent of gunner*bloom* and its obvious attraction to millennials seeking autonomy and purpose. Or it could simply remain a healthy, profitable outlier for T-shaped lawyers. Either way, Darryl and Sarah have neatly addressed the operational, training, and technological issues that would, on the face of it, seem to make a large, dispersed firm completely unworkable—guided not by the objective of giving lawyers more money or more prestige, but by simply making lawyers happier.

Somewhere Gunner Cooke is smiling.

CHAPTER 10
INKSTERS

Plug and Play Platforms, Part 2

Brian Inkster reminds me of what Elvis Costello would look like if he had become a lawyer: Inkster has an understated, new-wave coolness about him that fits nicely with his role as a legal entrepreneur—and he does kind of look like Elvis Costello in his prime. Kind of. The Shetland-born Scot started his legal career in 1991 at a traditional firm in Glasgow. Despite the distance from his birthplace—a good 90-minute flight away—he soon began fielding a steady stream of calls from the Shetland Islands. The appeal was obvious. He was one of them, but he also took a quicker and more efficient approach to solving their problems—something that few of the local Shetland lawyers did. Soon Brian was spending 100 percent of his time on legal files from Shetland—servicing all of them remotely from Glasgow: a rare occurrence in the early days of the internet, when lawyers were just beginning to understand email, and when Skype or online portals were only dreams.

By necessity, therefore, he was always looking at better ways to service Shetland clients, Brian told me from the modern environs of what he affectionately calls the "Inksterplex" in central Glasgow: a marvellously preserved Victorian building that nearly rivalled gunner*cooke*'s London location. "And despite the distance, I managed a general legal practice while building a specialization in crofting law.[23] This remote practice, where I didn't have the luxury of consistent face-to-face contact with my clients was the start of how we operate Inksters today," Brian told me in a soft brogue that I hoped I would still understand when I reviewed his interview tape back home. "Even today," he said, "No one is asking for Skype. They're happy to speak to a lawyer on the phone. Even still, we've just rolled out Odro Vision to facilitate online meetings for clients."

"Why leave and start up on your own?" I asked. The math wasn't adding up for me. Here was a guy with a full, self-supporting practice: something that traditional law firms drool over. The answer was that Brian simply got too busy to handle his workload and when he requested assistance that request fell upon deaf ears, although his firm assured him that help could be arranged as long as there was no cost to it. Brian was at a career crossroads: stay and not expand his practice, or leave and risk having his new practice fail.

Brian decided upon the latter and opened up a solo practice in 1999. "Initially I was just trying to find the best way to build up the Shetland practice. Then I started to get other work from different parts of Scotland. That opened my eyes to a new way of thinking." He had been thrust into an unconventional way of practicing by a geographically dispersed client base and he had made that practice successful. So, why not take it to the next level? Build an entire firm around a flexible and creative approach to legal services. This vision earned him the Managing Partner of the Year Award at the 2014 Law Awards of Scotland.

---

[23]   Crofting law deals with a wide variety of land rights particular to the highlands of Scotland.

Scotland is still clinging to archaic regulations that require only lawyers to own and manage law firms. This means that structurally, Inksters Solicitors is a solo practice with Brian himself personally liable for all costs and for finding any capital required to continue to build. And while Scotland has toyed with a limited form of alternative business structure (ABS), that legislation has yet to be proclaimed in force. For the time being, Brian does not have the option of attracting outside investment to his firm and he must find money through increased profits or through loans. Being a solo practice makes for a very lean decision-making team—a team of one. And as Inksters grows, Brian does less and less legal work. "My ultimate intention is to just manage the place."

I asked about succession and Brian acknowledges it's something that he will have to turn his mind to—"I'm still a young 49 year-old!" he quipped. And he will likely incorporate at some point as he believes that a corporate structure with good governance, systems, and processes will allow Inksters to survive well beyond the life of Brian. He's also hopeful that ABS will come to Scotland, thereby providing him with greater flexibility.

The Inksters model of practice, like gunner*cooke*, is loosely based on a hub-and-spoke mode of operation. Brian was an early adopter of cloud-based technology, moving wholeheartedly to the cloud in 2011; it seemed natural, given the remote work and the firm's intention to have dispersed operations. "We need everyone to have access to our IT from wherever they are—and with ease. We didn't find VPN to be terribly reliable," he said, referring to virtual private networking. "It really was a poor second cousin to a proper, cloud-based system where you're accessing a data centre. That move also allowed us to expand rapidly. On the back of that, we opened offices in Wick, Portree, and Forfar, in addition to our office in Inverness and our visiting base in Lerwick." Lawyers in these remote offices come into Glasgow when they can for social events and other firm functions, and Brian travels to each of the offices a few times a year. Nonetheless, Brian was quick to agree that it's a challenge to keep those lawyers feeling part of the Inksters community.

Cloud-based technology also allows Inksters lawyers in Glasgow to work from home if they so choose. Notwithstanding the benefits of commuting from the bedroom to the kitchen table, "certain types of work lends itself better to working together in the same place," Brian told me. "We needed a hub where people can work in teams and where the administrative teams would be settled." Those who choose to work at the Inksterplex do so in an open-space work environment—with no private offices, although private board rooms are available for confidential meetings or calls.

Despite being a solo practice with employees (lawyers and staff), Inksters also has also created a gunner*cooke*-type of arrangement by housing independent, self-employed lawyers, referred to as consultants. This is where Brian sees continuing growth. Like England, Scotland has a growing number of lawyers who want to discard the formal law firm apparatus and simply plug into the type of infrastructure that Brian is building.

This virtual, plug-and-play model interested me most and I asked Brian to walk me through it. Every new Inkster consultant is granted the use of space within the open office plan of the Inksterplex, along with full access to all IT systems, processes and precedents, as well as the ability to add materials to the firm website, in-house professional development programs, coverage in the global lawyers' insurance policy, and to get assistance with marketing. In return, Inksters takes a percentage of fees collected by the consultant. Consultants work any hours they choose, without any billing targets; keep in mind, however, if they don't work, they don't get paid. It's very much an "eat what you kill," model, although work does flow from the firm to consultants, and across consultants. The attraction is that consultants don't have the "hassle of operating or investing in the start-up costs of a law firm," Brian said. "And the lack of a partnership structure reduces office politics."

"The culture here makes me feel more valued," one consultant told me. "I don't have to justify to anyone why I'm going to my kids' events. There's also autonomy and mutual respect here. Brian is key to what is happening. He has a very clear vision."

"Could you leave now that you've been spoiled by this environment?" I asked.

She smiled. "It definitely puts Inksters in a very strong position, because it does make it hard for me to leave!"

While the model may work well for the consultants, all the costs and risk for this model fall solely and squarely on the shoulders of Brian Inkster. When I made this point, he shrugged at my comment. "It costs some money now, but I'll make it back in the long term. My share of the fee is not all going into my pocket. I'm investing a lot of that into the business to make it bigger and better," he said. "It's not about pocketing the money. It's about investing in the future of the business. If we're investing in things that make people better, then the firm benefits as a whole." Here again was yet another law firm leader talking about investing for the long term and forsaking short-term gain. In Brian's position, a small operation still finding its way, making long-term investments visible to consultants in particular is absolutely critical. Otherwise, at some point, consultants will begin to question the fee-sharing arrangement. So far, he has been successful in that regard because I did ask the question of consultants and often received some variation of the following comment, "I see how much time it would take me to do the things that Inksters is doing for me and there's value in that."

Part of Brian's latest line of investment has been in process engineering. He's been following the Hunoval and Seyfarth stories from across the Atlantic and is keen to see the same results at Inksters. Michelle Hynes was put in charge of process engineering in 2014 and, in what is becoming not at all unusual in the legal industry, she first connected with Brian Inkster on Twitter in 2009.

Michelle is excited by the possibilities at Inksters, possibilities that she can't see elsewhere in Scotland. "Now I can blaze the trail. Our focus is on legal engineering and building a long-term strategy for the firm with cost, culture, and technology driving what we wanted to do. But always, the client, both external and internal, is at the centre."

"Why do we do something? What do we want to get from it? What does the client get from it? It's not just about cutting costs. It's about creating a better client experience, through understanding, measuring, bench-marking, and analyzing things for client-service purposes, rather than for billing purposes." She sounded liked a mix of Matt Hunoval and Kim Craig, but with a Scottish accent. She nodded at my mention of Seyfarth and Hunoval. "We're bringing flavours of it here and trying to cover all our bases, but with balance. It helps with our evolution and for us it's all about evolution."[24]

---

[24] Before publication of this book, Michelle Hynes retired from Inksters due to health reasons.

Impressions

Inksters Solicitors was formed through a fortuitous mix of necessity (Shetland clients) and the intransigence of traditional law firms. If Brian Inkster had simply been just another good Glasgow lawyer, the Inksters platform would not exist. Brian knew from his experience with Shetland clients that a remote, flexible form of practice was palatable to clients and that technology already existed to make it work profitably—he simply took the next step. Moreover, he, like Sarah and Darryl at gunner*cooke*, understood the need to re-invest to keep the lawyers happy, and to constantly show them where their money was going. And he continually demonstrates that he is in service of the firm, rather than in service to himself.

It's hard not to notice the marked difference between Inksters operating in Scotland's traditional regulatory environment, and gunner*cooke*, which has taken advantage of England's more enlightened approach to legal service regulation. Both have found success with virtually (pun-intended) identical models, but one can't help but feel that Brian Inkster (and by extension a new generation of Scottish lawyers) is being unnecessarily held back from greater success by Scotland's antiquated regulatory regime, which encourages short-term thinking by forcing lawyers to fund all innovation from firm revenue or personal loans. One can imagine that Matt Hunoval would agree with this sentiment.

On the other hand, Inksters does provide a workable blueprint for lawyers in jurisdictions with similar regulations, provided they're willing to continually and selflessly reinvest in the new structure, and provided that the legal work of the entity is sufficiently spread across business sectors and practice areas so as to limit vulnerability to economic shocks.

CHAPTER 11

NOMADIC LAWYERS

Obelisk

Sometimes an outsider's perspective is what's needed to change the structure and operations of entities that provide legal services. I saw that previously with Riverview Law and it would play out again when Romanian-born, quadrilingual former journalist Dana Denis-Smith became a lawyer at the Magic Circle firm, Linklaters. It wasn't long before she began to see waste and inefficiencies, particularly in connection with human resources management and client relationships. "The lack of efficiency is not because clients aren't demanding it, it's because law firms aren't optimized as a business," she told me as we sipped lattes at a small café just steps from London's historic St John's Gate. "Law firms don't know how to deliver better because they don't know how to best manage their people. Internal operational matters are key and inefficiencies result from not aligning their people properly internally; your people may be very good and fast, but they're still inefficient."

She also was appalled by the blood-thirsty associate-to-partner tournament where lawyers who have the audacity to become pregnant or take time off for other reasons during prime tournament years were at an immediate disadvantage. To Dana, it seemed like a huge waste of good talent.

"So you decided to change that in your model?" I asked.

"The answer was sitting right there in front of me," she said. "Take people who want to work in a different way and pool their availability at scale to create a seamless process for the client."

"Somewhat like what Legal Process Outsourcers are doing," I ventured.

Dana bristled noticeably at the comparison. "No. We sit between the LPOs and the expert firms. Obelisk is a support offering for global clients. Do you need another pair of hands? Do you need reliable knowledge? We're not about cutting-edge transactions or the latest restructuring."

Dana wanted to create affordable quality for that type of work, without going offshore. "For the lawyers who join us," she continued, "we enable them to continue in a fully flexible way around everything else that is their priority—but wrapped in a community spirit so that everyone feels like they are part of something."

Dana launched Obelisk with 12 lawyers in July 2010—then became pregnant herself. If she didn't before, she now fully understood the situation of female lawyers on her team. Did I mention that women make up 76 percent of Obelisk's lawyers? "At first, our lawyers were mainly moms who wanted to come back to work, and to work as many or as few hours as they can, without feeling guilty about being bad mothers or feeling out of touch. However, we are increasingly seeing men embrace our model."

In February 2011 her daughter was born, giving Dana two babies to care for in less than a year. By May of that year she was able to refocus on Obelisk and provide an overflow solution for Goldman Sachs with multi-lingual, English-trained finance lawyers. That experience allowed her to refine her niche by providing lawyers with a wide variety of language abilities—something that most large law firms struggle with. That niche, however, still fits into Obelisk's four service lines: secondment (called "stand-in")[25]; fully home-based lawyer (called "stand-out"); an on-call service ("stand-by"); and a service that seconds people temporarily into a third party on behalf of a client (called "stand-off").[26] Obelisk's fees are fully flexible. "We use a variety of ways to price work: project-based or hourly rates."

Structurally, Obelisk is a limited company and since it's neither a law firm nor an alternative business structure it's not subject to the regulations that apply to those entities. "I don't want to be a provider in the traditional way," she said. "I'm a contrarian; I don't like to do whatever everyone else is doing—the opportunities are where other people don't go. We can be like Uber; we can challenge the regulations and create a truly unregulated market that helps businesses and lawyers."

Obelisk has an operations team of ten to coordinate the availability of now over 1,200 lawyers globally, all of whom are independent contractors; a performance manager captures all available hours in advance so that Obelisk knows its capacity well into the future and keeps in very close contact with its clients so it can forecast personnel needs and be ready for projects that happen months into the future. Geography creates no boundary for Obelisk. "We've had lawyers in Chile working for an Irish company, or lawyers in Europe working for businesses in Dubai

---

[25]   Dana Denis-Smith typically challenges a client who asks for a secondee to work at their offices. Is this a knee-jerk reaction to current workload, or is there a different and better way to handle the situation?

[26]   An example of this is when an Obelisk client enters into a joint venture arrangement with another company. The joint venture company will require some in-house legal expertise that the Obelisk client is unable to provide from its own resources.

or Singapore," she beamed. "Our goal is to continue removing barriers to work anywhere on the planet."

The flexible nature of Obelisk also means the company is constantly recruiting. "Every month we onboard 100 new lawyers from around the world and we've grown an average of 200 percent year-over-year for the last four years," Dana explained. In March 2017, Dana struck a deal with her former firm, a deal that allows Obelisk's pool of flexible lawyers to support Linklaters with its resourcing requirements: for example, an experienced Obelisk lawyer would help with a specific file on an ad hoc basis, or cover a leave of absence such as maternity leave and sabbaticals.

Obelisk's main office on St John's Lane is affectionately called "the Attic" and, like many attics, is relatively small. It's meant to act more as a hub, than as office space in the contemporary sense. And because Obelisk uses fully cloud-based technology, everyone on the internal operations team works from wherever they prefer—as do the lawyers. The day I was there, there were no lawyers present whatsoever and only a smattering of the support team.

I mentioned to her that some other players in this area have seen better and more innovative technology as a way to create differentiation and competitive advantage in the marketplace. "Given what we do," she responded, "there's no need for us to be super-sophisticated in creating technology for efficiency purposes. We use our clients' systems and our lawyers plug into that. Our focus is on creating technology that allows us to deliver better people solutions." Keeping a sense of belonging and community in such a diverse group spread around the world seemed like a tall order, one that would require some technological help. Dana acknowledged that challenge, telling me that "we've built a proprietary, web-based system to foster and connect our community, as well as to match lawyers when new jobs arise. Obelisk is not just about the work, it's about a sense of belonging, even if you don't work. So we're also building training courses, induction courses, mentorships, as well as upskilling people who want to go back to work full time."

"You expect people to leave you?" I asked.

"Of course! We want people to graduate from us. Obelisk is a landing pad for a life transition when work comes second," she said. "We've built something that allows lawyers to feel empowered and relevant for that period of their life. People move on from us and new clients have come from our alumni network."

LOD

For a still-nascent business model, the nomadic lawyer model has already seen a great deal of pick-up globally. I spoke with such operations in Africa, Australia, Asia, Canada, South America, and Europe, and they all have little problem drawing quality lawyers, and clients who want them. Moreover, there has already been a raft of consolidation in the industry with 2016 being a particularly banner year: Axiom (which declined to be part of this book) bought part of the Canadian operations of Cognition LLP as its first step into Canada; and a few months later, Deloitte acquired Toronto-based Conduit Law and continued Canadian operations as Deloitte Conduit Law LLP. The year 2016 also witnessed the global merger of the granddaddy of nomadic lawyering, UK-based Lawyers on Demand, with Australasian pioneer AdventBalance (itself a product of the 2012 merger of Advent Lawyer and Balance Legal). By the end of 2016, the name AdventBalance was retired, and now the merged firm simply called LOD boasts over 6,000 lawyers and eight offices: Sydney, Perth, Brisbane, Melbourne, Singapore, Hong

Kong, New York, and London. Not bad for a firm that, at the time of writing, was celebrating only its tenth birthday.

Lawyers on Demand (LOD) was spawned from the London firm, Berwin Leighton Paisner LLP (BLP), when Simon Harper, then a partner and leader of the firm's technology and media team, was on vacation. I caught up with Simon remotely, while he sat in the back of one of London's iconic black cabs. "If that makes the story sound better, go for it!" Simon responded when I said that I had heard that he came up with the idea for LOD while tanning on a nude beach. However, the actual story is much more mundane. Simon saw that corporate clients increasingly needed more legal work done, just not at BLP's pricing—and clients weren't able to do that type of work themselves. They needed a third option. "I was also hanging out with a very diverse group of people in technology, media, and the arts at the time—they all worked on a flexible basis. I had a hunch that lawyers might be interested in a similar model. But I didn't know how many of these types there would be."

Simon took his idea to the BLP partnership, who were surprisingly supportive; their only concern was quality. After Simon gave assurances that technical excellence would be paramount, the partners gave their blessing. It all seemed a bit too easy or just a bit too lucky for me. Simon was equally mystified and offered the suggestion that perhaps it was because it had never been done before (and at the time BLP had no formal process to deal with new structures), and because it carried a very low capital cost and little financial risk, it kind of flew under the radar at BLP. "There weren't any substantial objections," he recalled. "But a number of partners did ask me, 'Why are you doing this?'"

I asked him the same question.

"I just liked the idea! At the time it was a new way for lawyers to manage their own careers."

Simon ran two anonymous advertisements in the legal press to gauge market response. "That way if we didn't get any responses, no one would know." The ad, he told me, was written in a style that was very un-law firm, and loosely based on Scottish alternative rock band, Primal Scream's song, *Loaded*: apparently one of Simon's favourites.

"You know how it starts out?" he asked. But before I could answer he began singing out, "We want to be free. We want to be free to do what we want to do."

I had no idea what he was talking about.

But the advertisement elicited excellent talent and Simon found clients who were willing to use these lawyers. LOD never looked back. Technical excellence has remained at the heart of its recruitment policy with the typical LOD lawyer being a millennial who has 7 to 12 years of legal experience from a well-respected London, regional, or international firm. About 95 percent of LOD lawyers also have in-house experience and the male-female ratio of LOD lawyers runs at about 50-50. Each lawyer signs an agreement with LOD for each engagement where, among other things, the parties agree upon the weekly or daily rate to be paid to the lawyer. Like at Obelisk, LOD lawyers freely choose the files they want to work on. And while LOD may have been started by BLP, less than ten percent of its lawyers have ever worked for BLP. Lawyer engagements with LOD are also non-exclusive; lawyers are free to work elsewhere in addition to their LOD work. Simon told me that they lose very few LOD lawyers, but when they do, it's usually to a client, not a competitor.

In 2012, LOD was spun out from BLP and became a free-standing business, although it is still majority-owned by BLP. The spin-out allowed LOD to be more nimble and agile. It had grown too large to simply be just another department in the firm and had also begun doing work for other law firms; staying within BLP would limit its ability to grow that business.

I was curious about the fact that law firms would seek LOD lawyers.

"Firms prefer to use us on transactional work so they can scale quickly," Simon said. "They often ask us to build a team for some of the lower-level, routine work, so their associates can do the higher-value work." Using LOD allows law firms to reduce the cost of having a standing army of expensive associates.

Like the other dispersed entities I visited, LOD spends a great deal of time on what Simon calls *lawyer love*. "We have people whose only role is to be an account manager for the lawyers. Fielding a number of enquiries, from 'when and what is my next job?' to 'how do I get a new laptop?' We want and need to make our lawyers happy. So we also have social gatherings and they're able to take part in BLP training."

The London office of LOD is a stone's throw from London Bridge, and, as one may have guessed, small, yet modern enough to house some hot desk space for lawyers who want to work out of central London, as well as room for administrative staff. And similar to Obelisk's experience, LOD has found that technology and process improvement are less important in a business where lawyers are constantly being placed in different work environments and being asked to use different documentation and systems.

When I asked Simon if the market is getting crowded with the likes of other London firms such as Pinsent Masons and Allen & Overy creating their own nomadic lawyer networks, he was nonplussed. "The more organizations there are, the more it adds credibility to the model and the more it assists with normalizing clients to it. With more credibility and more normalization comes a new mentality. Soon we won't be seen as alternative legal providers—we'll just be part of the landscape."

Impressions

I had agreed with my wife to meet her across from St Paul's Cathedral at a casual wine bar, a spot midway between the offices of LOD and Obelisk. I arrived early, which gave me a chance to gather my thoughts. It was clear from the success of Obelisk, LOD, and others around the globe that the market for nomadic lawyers will only continue to grow. And why wouldn't it? It feeds on a millennial generation demanding more control over their careers, a profession that thoughtlessly sidelines scores of talented lawyers, and a marketplace that no longer views nomadic lawyers with suspicion—all with a low capital cost to entry.

In my mind, I ran through the absurdity of law firms spending tens (if not hundreds) of thousands of dollars training lawyers, then tossing them aside where they can be picked up by nomadic lawyer entities—who sell their services *back* to the same firms—or sell their services to clients of these firms. As legions of nomadic lawyers continue to grow, they will only put more, not less, stress on the traditional business model of many law firms. These nomadic models are not only siphoning away talent, they're siphoning away legal work. I wondered when traditional law firms would finally wake up to the fact that they were enabling new competitors and funding their own demise.

PART FOUR

CONCLUSIONS

CHAPTER 12

What Does It All Mean?

After my global walkabout in the legal innovation fog, I shut myself in my office in Toronto's Koreatown to make sense of my experiences and to think about what it could mean for the future of legal services, all the while struggling to ignore the temptation posed by the neighbourhood's Korean BBQ restaurants and the seemingly misplaced Chinese Dumpling House, two floors below.

The service providers I met took different approaches to the Great Legal Reformation (GLR). Some took advantage of legislative reform to create innovative structures that addressed unmet market needs, or to source capital, develop technology, or to apply new and diverse business expertise. It's no surprise therefore that the most exciting models are found in jurisdictions that permit alternative business structures. Their innovation and success highlight the important role that regulators can and should play in the GLR to foster breakthroughs and allow imaginative juxtapositions.

Others firms, hemmed in by antiquated regulations, focussed on a philosophy of continual improvement, using proven methods from other industries and recrafting them for legal services; methods that not only created new pricing dynamics, but also improved quality, efficiency, employee engagement, and client retention. Still others benefitted from a global legal marketplace that's filled with unhappy lawyers, and that trains, then discards, talented legal minds, using the competition's resources against it.

Most of these firms understand the power and opportunity of technology. It's obvious that technology permits dispersed, flexible working environments, increases accuracy and speed, and impacts pricing. What's less obvious is that a thoughtful use of technology can create new career paths, increase employee skill sets and engagement, as well as gather useful data for the entity and its clients.

At the helm of most of these service providers were leaders who treat their role as a full-time job. Leaders who understand that being trusted and respected are merely table stakes for leadership roles. They have the vision, patience, appetite, and willingness to adapt to the GLR. They're not leaders who are muddling through; nor are they leaders who make bold pronouncements for photo-ops or the occasional public relations bump, but then quickly move on to "the next big thing." They walk the talk on a daily basis and understand that transformation is a journey, not a destination—and they have imparted that ethos to their teams. They also have a rare sense of legacy: a desire to take the long view and build something that lasts long after they are gone.

At the heart of each leader's strategy is a vision to deliver legal services in a way that is different from that of its competitors. Inadvertently, this vision didn't just enhance client stickiness, it often created better team stickiness. These leaders also realized that their strategies required constant and consistent nurturing and investment. None of them believed that they had it all figured out; they were on a journey and there was still work to do.

Two other things struck me as I wrote this book. First, women at these entities were well represented—a very noticeable change from traditional law firms. As one lawyer told me, "it makes a huge difference having a majority of women in the office." And second, there was high energy at each entity. This energy or motivation was not centred on being the best paid, because I don't believe that any of the firms I interviewed were the top-paying firms in their jurisdictions. In fact, compensation was never mentioned as a driver of success or employee satisfaction at any of these firms, which suggests it's a false idol around which to build a successful legal services provider. Instead, motivation was driven by a sense of empowerment, a sense of doing something no one else was doing, and the belief that the entity was investing in the personal development of team members.

It became very apparent to me that human behaviour and human well-being are functions of the structure of the work environment. New structures and new work processes create different behaviours, and when behaviours change, clients receive a very different experience. And so often on my journeys, I heard Andrew Grech's voice in my head: "performance and engagement are driven by people understanding purpose, and feeling they are able to influence both the purpose and their ability to achieve that purpose." It made me wonder: if more legal services providers took this approach to their human resources, would mental wellness vastly improve among lawyers?

Further, as the Hunoval Law and Slaters stories indicate, adapting to the GLR does not make a firm bulletproof against economic realities or bad business decisions.

In an age of short attention spans, I'm often asked for a pithy sound bite that encapsulates the secret of success in the GLR. And while at first blush such a request sounds silly, many entities in this book used the same elements of success that some experts[27] have

---

[27] See Tony D'Emidio, David Dorton, and Ewan Duncan, "Service Innovation in a Digital World," *McKinsey Quarterly* (February 2015): http://www.mckinsey.com/business-functions/operations/our-insights/service-innovation-in-a-digital-world.

advocated for other service industries: *significant and consistent, long-term investment in client-centred service innovation (via technology or new processes) that creates unique client experiences.* The challenge for the entities in this book and for all those rushing into the legal innovation fog—and there seems to be no limit to the number of law firms now rushing to invest in legal tech products, IT consultancies, data analytics, artificial intelligence, and the like—will be to continue improving, learning and adjusting, because complacency will be the death of them.

The Road Ahead

The entities in this book illustrate how the GLR is driving fragmentation among legal service providers; for corporate clients, there has never been a more diverse selection of service providers from which to choose—legal services is no longer one size fits all. There is now a true legal services supply chain with different players performing different tasks.

The consumer legal market, however, still has room for improvement but it will need a catalyst: either regulatory reform of the kind I saw in Australia and in England, or seriously committed groups of lawyers willing to invest for the long term. Given that such a group of lawyers has failed to materialize to date, it's doubtful they will in the future, making regulatory reform the key to change in the consumer legal market. All that's missing in too many jurisdictions, is the will and courage to change, the absence of which will only further stimulate more combinations of DIY and legal technology to fill the void. Add in the growth of block-chain and smart contracts, which will further impact the role of lawyers, and the legal profession stands to lose opportunities to assist large portions of the consumer market.

But no matter what the legal tech cool kids come up with in the future, the GLR will not eliminate lawyers from all legal services, but it will force us to see legal services through a different lens. A lens that focuses on output, rather than input: a lens that forces providers to assemble the best combination of people, process, and technology so as to achieve that output, regardless of the weighting within the mix. Interestingly, there's nothing earth-shattering about this approach; it was used by the first peoples of North America for centuries: "success for them wasn't about a lone brave out on his or her own, but the careful study of weather patterns and the local environment, monitoring the habits of their prey and the trailblazing activities conducted by the entire tribe working together."[28] Put another way, the GLR will force many legal service providers to view legal services as a team sport, where lawyers will simply be specialists, filling gaps that can't otherwise be addressed by technology and workflow. Team members without legal training won't do what lawyers do, and the lawyers won't do what other team members do; however, neither group will find success alone. A team, or enterprise, approach to legal services naturally creates a far more diverse set of opportunities and career paths than those found at traditional law firms: something that's crucial for millennials who crave participation, contribution, and purpose.

This team sport metamorphosis will also drive subtle changes to the nomenclature used to describe personnel working at legal services entities. The distasteful binary distinction of lawyer/non-lawyer will disappear from our lexicon and be replaced with "team

---

[28]   Kim Tasso, *Rainmakers and Trailblazers* (Legal Monitor, 2014) ix.

member" or "legal services worker"; and within that term will be sub-categories of managers, legal technicians, support workers, lawyers, and so on. For many legal service providers, lawyers will be to the legal services industry what pilots are to the airline industry— an important piece of the puzzle, but not the entire puzzle.

Over the coming decades, the talent mix within legal services providers will continue to adjust as the cool kids relentlessly experiment with legal technology, reducing the need for large masses of lawyers. How can it not? Technology gets better, not worse, giving legal services workers, who did not go to law school, the ability to do more work, with greater accuracy and in less time, from anywhere on the planet. This will allow legal service providers to look at scale in a completely different way; scale no longer means hiring more (expensive) lawyers, since a legal solution no longer involves something that can only be delivered by a lawyer. Scale will be achieved through technology, workflow, and process, with lawyers being hired only when absolutely necessary. Just as economists once spoke of a jobless recovery from the financial crisis of 2008, lawyer-less growth is not only imaginable, it's now possible.

Lawyer-less growth means that job creation in the legal services sector will favour those who did not invest in a law school education but bring other valuable skills to the table. It will also favour those who can skill-up through workflow and technology to provide a certain layer of legal service. As a result, many incumbent legal service providers will start to more aggressively trim their high-priced legal talent and replace it, wherever possible, with smart, engaged employees having less intensive legal training but fully supported by workflow and technology.

Legal services as a team sport will require a dramatic re-thinking of compensation, career paths, career advancement key performance indicators and hiring practices at incumbent legal service entities, and will thus ultimately force structural reform. The partnership structure and its associate-to-partner tournament cannot be adapted to a model of service delivery that doesn't rely heavily upon lawyers. In a team sport model, there needs to be attractive opportunities for those who aren't lawyers, forcing a move to a corporatized structure. The inability of the old model to adapt to a new reality also means that success will favour new players: those unburdened by legacy constraints.

This shift in human resource allocation will require sophisticated business management skills that are currently not part of a lawyer's skill set. As Ken Grady told me during one conversation, "Law firms are not good training grounds for leaders. They're not structured to build CEOs like corporations are, where executives move through different areas and receive different levels of responsibility. In law firms, few partners have training or experience as leaders." It stands to reason therefore, that lawyers will also eventually be trimmed from law firm management, because the fundamentals of a successful legal services entity will transcend pure legal acumen and require skills that very few lawyers possess.

The discussions throughout this book dovetail neatly with the Susskinds' seemingly audacious conclusion in *The Future of the Professions*: "the traditional professions will be dismantled, leaving most (but not all) professionals to be replaced by less expert people and high-performing systems."[29] This is no longer (if it ever was) conjecture or speculation; I've given readers a glimpse at how this is starting to become a reality in legal services. And there's no reason for this process to reverse itself or

---

[29]   Richard Susskind and Daniel Susskind, *The Future of the Professions* (Oxford University Press, 2015).

SUGGESTED READING

BOOKS

Ronald Baker, *Implementing Value Pricing: A Radical Business Model for Professional Firms* (Wiley, 2010)

George Beaton & Imme Kaschner, *Remaking Law Firms: Why and How* (American Bar Association, 2016)

Mark Cohen, *More Essays on Legal Delivery* (Legal Business World, 2017)

Jeena Cho and Karen Gifford, *The Anxious Lawyer* (American Bar Association, 2016)

Casey Flaherty, *Unless You Ask* (Association of Corporate Counsel, 2016)

Jordan Furlong, *Law is a Buyer's Market: Building a Client-first Law Firm* (L21 Press, 2017)

Joanna Goodman, *Robots in Law: How Artificial Intelligence is Transforming Legal Services* (Ark Conferences Ltd., 2016)

Mary Lacity, Leslie Willcocks and Andrew Burgess *The Rise of Legal Services Outsourcing: Risk and Opportunity*, (Bloomsbury, 2015)

Patrick Lamb, *Alternative Fee Arrangements: Value Fees and the Changing Legal Market* (Ark Publishing, 2010)

Patrick Lamb, *Alternative Fees for Litigators and Their Clients* (American Bar Association, 2014)

Chrissie Lightfoot, *Tomorrow's Naked Lawyer: NewTech, NewHuman, NewLaw* (Ark Conferences Ltd. 2014)

Bruce MacEwen, *Growth is Dead: Now What?* (Adam Smith, Esq., 2013)

Bruce MacEwen, *A New Taxonomy: The Seven Law Firm Business Models* (Adam Smith, Esq., 2014)

Bruce MacEwen, *Tomorrowland: Scenarios for Law Firms Beyond the Horizon* (Adam Smith, Esq., 2017)

Stephen Mayson, *Making Sense of Law Firms* (Blackstone Press Ltd. 1997)

Stephen Mayson, *Law Firm Strategy* (Oxford University Press 2007)

Noel Semple, *Legal Services Regulation at the Crossroads* (Elgaronline, 2015)

Sylvia Hodges Silverstein and Tom Sager, *Legal Procurement Handbook* (Buying Legal Council, 2015)

Asheem Singh, *The Moral Marketplace: How Mission-driven Millennials and Social Entrepreneurs are Changing Our World* (Policy Press University of Bristol, 2017)

Laura Snyder, *Democratizing Legal Services: Obstacles and Opportunities* (Lexington, 2016)

Laura Snyder, *Modernizing Legal Services: Will the US be Left Behind?* (Lexington, 2017)

Hilary Sommerlad, Sonia Harris-Short, Steven Vaughn and Richard Young (Editors), *The Futures of Legal Education and the Legal Profession* (Hart Publishing, 2015)

Richard Susskind, *The Future of Law* (Oxford University Press 1996)

Richard Susskind, *The End of Lawyers?* (Oxford University Press 2008)

Richard Susskind, *Tomorrow's Lawyers* 2nd ed. (Oxford University Press 2017)

Richard Susskind and Daniel Susskind, *The Future of the Professions* (Oxford University Press 2015)

REPORTS

Altman Weil, Inc., *Law Firms in Transition Studies*, 2009 to date

American Bar Association, *Report on the Future of Legal Services in the United States*, 2016

American Bar Association, *The Path to Lawyer Well-Being: Practical Recommendations for Positive Change (The Report of the National Task Force on Lawyer Well-Being)*, 2017

Aly R. Haji, Karl J. Moore, and Mike Ross, *The Illusion of Innovation in Canadian Law Firms*, 2017

Canadian Bar Association, *Legal Futures Initiative Reports*, 2013 to date

Deloitte Canada, *Canadian Legal Landscape*, 2017

The Law Society of England and Wales, *Capturing Technological Innovation in Legal Services*, 2017

The Law Society of England and Wales, *The Future of Legal Services*, 2016

The Law Society of New South Wales, *The Future of Law and Innovation in the Profession*, 2017

The Law Society of Upper Canada, *Mental Health Strategy Task Force Report*, 2016

The Law Society of Western Australia, *Report on Psychological Distress and Depression in the Legal Profession*, 2011

Megan Seto, "Killing Ourselves: Depression as an Institutional, Workplace and Professionalism Problem," (2012) *UWO Journal of Legal Studies* 5

The National Self-Representative Litigants Project (Canada), 2013 to date

Thomson Reuters and Georgetown Law School, *Annual Reports on the State of the Legal Market* (USA), 2010 to date

Thomson Reuters and Melbourne Law School, *Annual Reports on the State of the Legal Market* (Australia), 2010 to date

WEB-BASED RESOURCES

Website Name	Web Address
3 Geeks and a Law Blog	http://www.geeklawblog.com/
Adam Smith, Esq.	http://www.adamsmithesq.com/
Amazing Firms, Amazing Practices	http://www.gerryriskin.com/
Artificial Lawyer	https://www.artificiallawyer.com/
Asia Law Portal	https://asialawportal.com/
Association of Corporate Counsel	http://www.acc.com/
At the Intersection	http://www.pamwoldow.com/
Attorney at Work	http://www.attorneyatwork.com/
Corporate Legal Operations Consortium	https://cloc.org/
David J. Bilinsky Thoughtful Legal Management	http://thoughtfullaw.com/
In Search of Perfect Client Service	http://www.patrickjlamb.com/
John Chisholm Blog	http://www.chisconsult.com/
John Flood's Random Academic Thoughts	http://www.johnflood.com/blog/
Jordan Furlong Law 21	http://www.law21.ca/blog
Laura Snyder	www.notjustforlawyers.com
Legal Evolution	http://www.legalevolution.org/
Legal Futures	http://www.legalfutures.co.uk/blog
Legal Mosaic	http://legalmosaic.com/blog/
Legal Tech Blog	http://legal-tech-blog.de/
Prism Legal	http://www.prismlegal.com/wordpress/
Remaking Law Firms The Dialogue Blog	http://www.remakinglawfirms.com/dialogue/
LawSites by Robert Ambrogi	http://www.lawsitesblog.com/
Seytlines	http://www.seytlines.com/
Stephen Mayson Occasional Thoughts	https://stephenmayson.com/occasional-thoughts/
The Algorithmic Society (tagged Future of Law)	https://medium.com/the-algorithmic-society/tagged/future-of-law
The Intelligent Challenge	http://intelligentchallenge.com/
Validatum	http://www.validatum.com/articles

AUDIO RESOURCE

The go-to podcast that interviews leading thinkers in this area is:

Building NewLaw, downloadable from: https://www.countertax. ca/bnlpodcast

ACKNOWLEDGMENTS

To state the obvious, this book could not have been completed without the persons in it agreeing to sit down and spend time with me; a huge amount of thanks goes out to them for their time and patience. Thanks to Ken Grady for his comments on Lean and law firm management, and to Tahlia Gordon and Steve Mark of Creative Consequences, for their comments on ABS in Australia, and to Stephen Mayson for his comments on ABS in the UK; hopefully I got it right now, but any errors are on me. Heartfelt thanks to Stephen Allen, Debbie Allen, Barney Allen, and Harvey Allen (and Bertie!) for allowing Yvonne and me to stay at their beautiful home outside London. To the students of Law 2025 at the University of Calgary Law School: you give me new energy every time I teach!

Finally, every author needs super editors. There's so much going on in any book that, after being immersed in it for long periods of time, authors become blind to the obvious— and to the immaterial. So, I'm most grateful to Tim Brandhorst and Victoria Barclay for their insight, comments, and suggestions which have made this a much better book! All errors are mine. However, I do blame all weird non-capitalization on the Chicago Manual of Style!

ABOUT THE AUTHOR

Author Photo Credit:
Phil Brown,
Twitter @psuba98

Mitchell Kowalski is the inaugural Gowling WLG Visiting Professor in Legal Innovation at the University of Calgary Law School, the legal innovation columnist for the National Post, and a consultant for in-house legal departments and law firms on the redesign of legal service delivery. He was formerly a partner at one of the world's largest law firms, and has also served as in-house legal counsel. He is a Fastcase 50 Global Legal Innovator and the author of the critically acclaimed book, *Avoiding Extinction: Reimagining Legal Services for the 21st Century*. Follow him on Twitter @mekowalski or visit www.kowalski.ca.